TIKTOK COOKBOOK 2025

Unlock Your Culinary Creativity: The Ultimate Guide to Delicious Recipes and Gaining Online Influence

ANNALIE DACHS

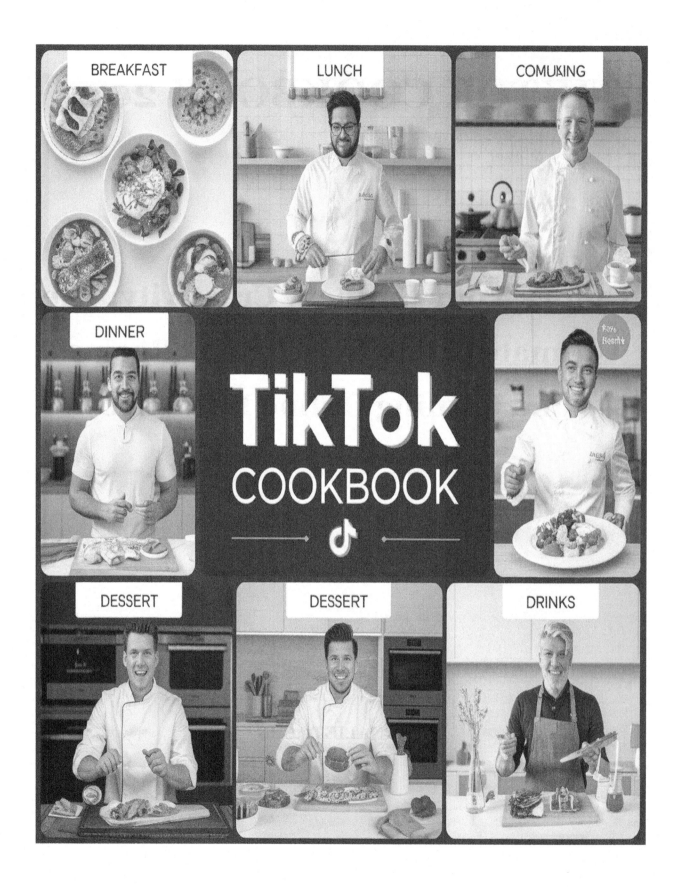

BREAKFAST

LUNCH

COMUKING

DINNER

TikTok
COOKBOOK

DESSERT

DESSERT

DRINKS

CREAMY GARLIC PASTA

COPYRIGHT © BY ANNALIE DACHS

DISCLAIMER

The information contained in this book, "TikTok Cookbook," is for general informational purposes only. The author and publisher have made every effort to ensure that the content provided is accurate and up-to-date. However, the author and publisher do not warrant the completeness, reliability, or accuracy of the information, and they disclaim all responsibility for any loss, injury, claim, liability, or damage of any kind resulting from any errors or omissions in the content of this book.

The recipes provided in this book are intended for personal use and enjoyment. The author and publisher are not responsible for any adverse effects or consequences that may arise from the use of the recipes or the ingredients used. It is the reader's responsibility to exercise caution, follow safe cooking practices, and consider any dietary restrictions or allergies when preparing and consuming the recipes.

LIABILITY

The author and publisher of this book, "TikTok Cookbook," shall not be held liable for any direct, indirect, incidental, special, or consequential damages arising out of the use of the information or recipes provided in this book. The author and publisher disclaim any liability for errors or omissions in the content and for any actions taken or not taken based on the information or recipes contained herein.

Before attempting any of the recipes or activities described in this book, it is recommended that readers consult with a qualified professional, such as a doctor or nutritionist, to address any individual concerns or specific dietary needs.

FOREWORD BY COPELAND ANDERSON

When I was first invited to write the foreword for the 2023 edition of TikTok Cookbook, I was thrilled. As a culinary enthusiast, I've always been fascinated by how food brings people together. But what truly amazed me was witnessing TikTok's role in revolutionizing the way we share and discover recipes. Fast forward to 2024, and that impact has only grown. Now, with this new edition updated for 2025, the cookbook takes TikTok's culinary magic to the next level.

Imagine a platform where a single video can inspire millions to rush to their kitchens, eager to recreate a viral recipe. That's what TikTok has done. In a world of shrinking attention spans, it has somehow managed to bring us all back to the table—one bite-sized video at a time. With quick flicks and creative twists, TikTok has birthed a new wave of home cooks who aren't just following trends but creating them.

This edition of **TikTok Cookbook** goes beyond those viral moments you might recognize. Within these pages, you'll find an expertly curated collection of TikTok's most iconic recipes, now refined for the everyday cook. The author has done an incredible job translating the vibrant energy and creativity of TikTok into a format that's both practical and delightful, capturing the essence of what makes these viral dishes so special.

What I love most about this book is how it invites readers on a journey. You'll traverse different cuisines and flavors, from playful appetizers to indulgent desserts that will make your taste buds sing. Each recipe is more than just a list of ingredients and steps—it's an invitation to experiment, to play with your food, and to create something truly your own.

In today's fast-paced digital world, this cookbook reminds us that food is still about connection—whether it's a family meal, a dinner party, or just you alone in your kitchen trying a fun new dish. It's about savoring the process, getting creative with flavors, and, above all, sharing those moments with others. TikTok's cooking community embodies this spirit, and this book captures it beautifully.

Whether you're a seasoned chef looking for fresh inspiration or a kitchen newbie ready to tackle your first viral recipe, **TikTok Cookbook 2025** has something for you. The recipes are approachable, the instructions are clear, and the results? Absolutely delicious. With this book as your guide, you'll not only master TikTok's most beloved dishes but also discover the joy of creating something that's uniquely yours.

So grab your apron, put on your favorite playlist, and get ready to whip up meals that will wow your family, friends, and maybe even your TikTok followers. This isn't just another cookbook—it's a gateway to a global community of food lovers, all connected by the simple joy of a good meal.

Welcome to the adventure.
Copeland Anderson

TABLE OF CONTENTS

INTRODUCTION

TikTok isn't just a social media platform; it's a cultural phenomenon that has redefined the way we experience food. What started as a space for dance challenges and viral trends has quickly evolved into a global stage for culinary creativity. From home cooks testing out new ideas in their kitchens to professional chefs revealing their trade secrets, TikTok's fast-paced, visually-driven format has transformed how we discover, share, and fall in love with food.

In a world where attention spans are short, TikTok has proven that a 60-second video can spark a craving, launch a food trend, or even inspire millions to try something new in their kitchens. Whether it's the perfect fold on a tortilla wrap hack or a mesmerizing dessert that seems too beautiful to eat, TikTok has given food enthusiasts a unique way to connect through flavor and creativity.

In this introduction, we'll dive into the rise of TikTok as a culinary force, exploring how it has reshaped food culture and brought short-form video recipes to the forefront of the cooking world. TikTok isn't just about following trends—it's about making them, and this book is your guide to tapping into that energy and bringing those viral dishes to life in your own kitchen.

The Rise of Culinary Content on TikTok

TikTok's meteoric rise to fame can be credited to its ability to hook users with fast, captivating videos. Originally known for dance challenges and lip-syncing, the platform quickly evolved to include a diverse range of content, with cooking emerging as one of its most popular categories. Food creators were quick to spot the platform's potential, transforming TikTok into a playground for culinary innovation. They saw the opportunity to not just share their passion for cooking but also to experiment with creative, bite-sized recipe formats that could inspire millions with just a few swipes.

The Influence of TikTok on Food Culture

TikTok has transformed food culture, reshaping culinary trends and influencing how people approach cooking. Through its quick, visually engaging videos, the platform has made cooking more accessible, exciting, and fun for cooks of all skill levels. TikTok has broken down the traditional barriers of the culinary world, empowering anyone with a smartphone to become a food creator, whether they're whipping up gourmet dishes or sharing simple, everyday meals.

The platform's signature recipe format—short, step-by-step videos—has made it easier for viewers to follow along and recreate dishes in their own kitchens. This bite-sized content has struck a chord, especially with younger generations who crave concise, visually captivating experiences. Beyond just recipes, TikTok has fostered a thriving community where experimentation and culinary exploration are celebrated, bringing together food lovers from all walks of life.

Exploring the Power of Short-Form Video Recipes

Short-form video recipes have become the heart of TikTok's culinary world, offering creators a powerful way to share their passion in just a few seconds. With the swipe of a finger, you're transported into kitchens around the globe, where home cooks and professional chefs alike showcase their skills, reveal hidden cooking techniques, and plate up dishes that leave you hungry for more. The magic lies in the brevity—these bite-sized videos are perfect for today's fast-paced, shareable world.

TikTok's recipe videos captivate with their visual appeal, using overhead shots, mouthwatering close-ups, and time-lapse sequences to turn the cooking process into a work of art. The simplicity of text overlays and captions guides viewers effortlessly through each step, ensuring the recipes are not only easy to follow but also incredibly engaging. This concise yet vivid approach has revolutionized how recipes are shared, making cooking feel less intimidating and more accessible to everyone.

Beyond just being a platform for sharing recipes, TikTok has ignited some of the most memorable food trends of recent years. Who could forget the viral wave of whipped coffee or the feta pasta that seemed to take over everyone's feed? These trends go beyond the kitchen—they create a sense of connection, where millions of users join in, experiment, and add their own flair. It's not just about cooking; it's about being part of something bigger, a shared experience that spans continents.

As TikTok continues to evolve, it offers an exciting opportunity for seasoned chefs and aspiring home cooks alike. It's a space where creativity knows no bounds, where you can try new things, inspire others, and redefine what it means to share a meal in the digital age. With the rise of short-form video, we've entered a new era of cooking content—one that's not only visually stunning but also deeply engaging and inclusive.

CHAPTER ONE

Getting Started with TikTok Cooking

TikTok has rapidly become a culinary playground, where short-form videos and viral trends have redefined how we cook, share, and experience food. From irresistible recipes to creative cooking hacks, it's a space where anyone—from seasoned chefs to first-time home cooks—can shine. In this chapter, we'll explore the dynamic world of TikTok cooking, unpacking the recipe formats that make it so engaging, the key ingredients for creating content that captivates, and the strategies for building a successful TikTok cooking account. Get ready to transform your kitchen into the next viral sensation!

Mastering TikTok's Recipe Format

TikTok's recipe format is as fast-paced and innovative as the platform itself, offering creators the perfect canvas to showcase their culinary skills in just 15 to 60 seconds. These bite-sized videos are engineered to captivate, using sharp visuals, quick cuts, and dynamic storytelling to turn even the simplest dish into a must-try sensation. Whether it's a drool-worthy dessert, a savory main course, or a trending beverage, TikTok recipes are designed to stop viewers mid-scroll and inspire them to recreate the magic in their own kitchens. As TikTok continues to evolve, we're seeing more creators push the boundaries with AI-generated food ideas, interactive cooking challenges, and even augmented reality recipe guides—proof that the future of food content is here, and it's exciting.

Key Elements of Engaging Cooking Content

Creating standout TikTok cooking content means mastering a few key elements that capture attention and keep viewers coming back for more. First, visuals are everything. High-quality footage, well-lit kitchens, and visually striking plating can make or break your video's appeal. Investing in good lighting, experimenting with camera angles, and even using trending visual effects or transitions can elevate your content to the next level, ensuring every step of your recipe shines.

Text overlays and captions are just as vital in engaging viewers. Use TikTok's text tools to display ingredients, measurements, and helpful tips in real-time, making your videos easy to follow. Pair this with snappy captions, clever humor, or personal anecdotes to give your content a relatable, human touch. Future-forward creators are even starting to incorporate interactive polls, augmented reality elements, and AI-powered features, allowing them to engage audiences in fresh, exciting ways. Staying on top of these trends will keep your content relevant and highly shareable in the fast-paced world of TikTok.

Navigating TikTok's Cooking Challenges and Trends

TikTok thrives on viral challenges, and the culinary world is no exception. Participating in cooking challenges is one of the best ways to gain exposure, tap into the community, and showcase your creativity. Whether you're recreating a trending dish or putting your own spin on a popular recipe, these challenges offer a golden opportunity to stand out and attract new followers.

Staying ahead of the latest cooking trends on TikTok is crucial for success. Regularly explore the "For You" page to discover new food trends and follow top food creators to keep your content fresh. Don't forget to tap into trending hashtags—they can significantly boost your discoverability and help your videos reach a broader audience. Engaging with the TikTok cooking community is equally important. Comment on videos, participate in discussions, and collaborate with other creators to build meaningful connections. These interactions not only increase visibility but open the door for collaborations, taking your TikTok cooking account to new heights.

Setting Up Your TikTok Cooking Account

Your TikTok profile is your first impression, so make it count. Start by choosing a username that reflects your cooking niche or personal brand—something catchy, memorable, and easy to find. Next, craft a bio that quickly introduces who you are and what sets your cooking apart, whether it's your signature style, favorite cuisine, or expertise. Keep it concise but impactful. If you have a blog or website, be sure to include a link—it's a great way to drive traffic to your other platforms and expand your reach beyond TikTok. With a clear, compelling profile, you'll draw in followers who are excited to see more of your culinary creations.

Building a Follower Base

Building a strong follower base on TikTok demands both consistency and engagement. Stick to a regular posting schedule to create a routine for your audience and keep them coming back for more. Leverage trending sounds, songs, and effects to make your videos resonate with current trends and increase their shareability. Diversify your content with different formats—step-by-step tutorials, quick cooking tips, or behind-the-scenes glimpses—to appeal to various viewer preferences.

Engagement is key to fostering a loyal community. Actively respond to comments, address questions, and give shoutouts to user-generated content related to your recipes. Encourage viewers to duet or stitch your videos to boost interaction and collaboration. Show genuine appreciation for your followers by offering valuable content—educational tips, inspiring ideas, and helpful advice. By creating a dynamic and interactive presence, you'll build a dedicated following that's excited to engage with your culinary content.

Leveraging Hashtags and Trends for Visibility

Hashtags are crucial for boosting the visibility of your TikTok cooking content. Start by researching and using popular hashtags related to cooking, recipes, and food trends to ensure your videos appear in relevant searches and attract users interested in those topics. Incorporate these hashtags thoughtfully into your captions to extend your reach.

Beyond leveraging established hashtags, create a unique hashtag for your brand or cooking style. Encourage your viewers to use this hashtag when they try your recipes or share their culinary creations. This not only helps you track user-generated content but also builds a stronger community and fosters a sense of belonging among your followers.

To further enhance your visibility, stay on top of trending hashtags and challenges within the TikTok cooking community. Engaging with these trends exposes your content to a larger audience and positions you as an active participant in the community. Stay flexible and ready to experiment with new trends as they arise—they can offer valuable opportunities for growth and exposure.

Remember, consistent posting, active engagement, and staying current with cooking trends are key to growing your TikTok presence. Embrace TikTok's dynamic environment, let your cooking passion shine, and build genuine connections with your audience. With dedication and creativity, you'll carve out a prominent space in the vibrant world of TikTok cooking.

CHAPTER TWO

Mastering TikTok Cooking Techniques

In the fast-paced world of social media, TikTok has emerged as a powerful platform for culinary content. With its short-form video format and engaging features, TikTok has revolutionized the way people share and consume recipes. Chapter 2 of this comprehensive guide aims to help you master TikTok cooking techniques, offering a range of quick and easy recipes for beginners, as well as tips to level up your culinary skills.

Understanding TikTok's Recipe Format

TikTok's recipe format is unique and tailored to capture viewers' attention within a short span of time. It typically consists of a series of short clips that demonstrate each step of the cooking process. These videos are often accompanied by catchy music and on-screen text to guide the viewers through the recipe. Understanding this format is essential to create engaging and captivating cooking content on TikTok.

The Basics of TikTok Recipe Videos

When creating TikTok recipe videos, clarity and visual appeal are key. Keep your videos short and to the point, demonstrating each step clearly so viewers can easily follow along. Break the recipe into manageable segments, using visual cues to spotlight essential ingredients and techniques. Leverage TikTok's editing tools—such as jump cuts and smooth transitions—to keep your content dynamic and engaging. By focusing on concise instructions and eye-catching visuals, you'll capture your audience's attention and make your recipes both accessible and compelling.

Key Elements of Engaging Cooking Content

To captivate your audience on TikTok, focus on a few essential elements. First, let your personality and passion for cooking shine through—viewers connect with genuine enthusiasm, so don't be afraid to showcase your unique flair. Next, prioritize the visual appeal of your dishes. Use vibrant ingredients, artful plating, and inventive presentation techniques to make your recipes stand out and tempt viewers. Finally, keep the pace lively and energetic. TikTok thrives on fast-moving, dynamic content, so maintain a brisk tempo to keep your audience engaged and entertained from start to finish.

Navigating TikTok's Cooking Challenges and Trends

TikTok is always abuzz with cooking challenges and trending recipes, offering fantastic opportunities to connect with the community and boost your visibility as a food creator. Stay alert for trending hashtags and dive into relevant challenges to showcase your culinary skills and creativity. Additionally, explore popular food trends and put your own unique twist on them. By adding a personal touch or creative spin to these viral trends, you'll not only stand out but also attract a larger audience eager to see your take on the latest culinary fads.

Quick and Easy Recipes for Beginners

For beginners, TikTok offers a wealth of quick and easy recipes that can be whipped up with minimal effort. These recipes are perfect for those who are just starting their culinary journey or looking for convenient meal options. Chapter 2 delves into three main categories of beginner-friendly recipes.

Whip It Up: Fast and Flavorful 15-Minute Meals

In this section, you'll find a curated selection of recipes that can be whipped up in just 15 minutes. Perfect for those with hectic schedules or anyone craving a homemade meal without hours spent in the kitchen, these dishes offer a winning combination of flavor and speed. From satisfying stir-fries to savory pasta creations, each recipe is crafted to deliver maximum taste and convenience, making it easier than ever to enjoy a delicious meal on the go.

One-Pot Wonders: Effortless and Delicious Recipes

One-pot meals are perfect for those who want to simplify their cooking routine and reduce cleanup. This section features a selection of recipes that require just one pot or pan, making meal preparation both efficient and enjoyable. From comforting soups to rich stews, each recipe is designed to deliver a range of delicious flavors while keeping the cooking process straightforward and stress-free.

Kitchen Hacks: Time-Saving Tips and Tricks

Mastering kitchen hacks can transform your cooking routine, making it more efficient and enjoyable. In this section, we dive into TikTok-inspired kitchen hacks that streamline your culinary process and save you precious time. These clever tricks range from quick methods for peeling garlic to innovative ways to cut fruits, all designed to make your cooking experience smoother and more enjoyable.

One popular TikTok hack is using the microwave to soften butter quickly. Instead of waiting for butter to come to room temperature, simply place it in a microwave-safe bowl and heat in short intervals until it's soft and spreadable. This trick is a game-changer when you're in a rush to bake cookies or prepare a cake.

Another handy tip is the "eggshell removal trick." If you've ever struggled with bits of eggshell in your batter, try this: wet your finger and gently touch the eggshell pieces. The moisture will make the shell cling to your finger, making removal easy and hassle-free.

TikTok also offers smart ways to handle fruits and vegetables efficiently. For instance, peel ginger quickly by scraping it with a spoon instead of using a knife. To remove kiwi skin, cut off the ends, insert a spoon between the flesh and skin, and scoop out the fruit effortlessly.

And if you're tired of slicing cherry tomatoes individually, TikTok has a time-saving solution. Place a bunch of tomatoes between two plates, apply gentle pressure, and run a knife through the gap. This method slices all the tomatoes at once, making prep work faster and simpler.

These are just a few of the ingenious hacks you'll find on TikTok. As you explore, you'll uncover even more tricks to revolutionize your kitchen routine and enhance your cooking experience.

Leveling Up: Intermediate TikTok Recipes

Now that you've mastered the basics of TikTok cooking, it's time to elevate your skills and explore more complex and adventurous recipes. Chapter 2 dives into a curated collection of intermediate TikTok recipes designed to challenge your culinary prowess and broaden your flavor horizons. Prepare to tackle exciting new dishes that will push your creativity and technique, offering a deeper dive into the vibrant world of TikTok-inspired cuisine.

Elevating Basic Dishes with Unique Twists

In this section, you'll discover how to transform everyday dishes into extraordinary culinary creations with creative and unexpected twists. TikTok is teeming with innovative ideas for turning classics like grilled cheese sandwiches, pizza, and salads into gourmet delights. Learn the art of flavor pairing, experiment with unconventional ingredients, and explore unique combinations that will not only surprise your taste buds but also captivate your viewers. Get ready to elevate your everyday meals into memorable gourmet experiences that leave everyone craving more.

Exploring International Flavors through TikTok

One of the most exciting aspects of TikTok cooking is its ability to introduce you to diverse culinary traditions from around the world. Explore the platform's vast collection of international recipes and embark on a virtual culinary journey. From Mexican street tacos to Japanese sushi rolls, you'll find step-by-step videos that guide you through the intricacies of each cuisine. Embrace the flavors, techniques, and cultural nuances of global cuisine as you expand your culinary repertoire.

Perfecting Plating and Presentation for Visual Appeal

In TikTok cooking, presentation is key to capturing viewers' attention and creating a memorable visual experience. This section delves into the art of plating and presentation, offering essential tips and techniques to make your dishes as visually appealing as they are delicious. Learn how to arrange ingredients beautifully, use garnishes to add vibrant pops of color, and experiment with textures and heights to craft plates that impress and delight.

TikTok is brimming with visually stunning food videos that provide endless inspiration. Here, you'll discover how to incorporate these presentation techniques into your own creations, elevating your dishes to new heights and ensuring they stand out in a sea of content.

As you continue your TikTok cooking journey, this chapter equips you with the skills to navigate the platform with confidence. From mastering TikTok's unique recipe format to creating engaging and aesthetically pleasing content, you'll be well-prepared to showcase your culinary talents.

Progressing through your TikTok adventure, you'll explore intermediate recipes that challenge and expand your cooking skills. Learn to infuse everyday dishes with creative twists, discover international flavors, and perfect the art of presentation.

TikTok has transformed the way we approach cooking and recipe sharing. Its dynamic short-form videos make cooking accessible and enjoyable for everyone. By mastering TikTok cooking techniques, you'll not only enhance your culinary abilities but also inspire and captivate others with your unique creations.

In the upcoming chapter, "Exploring TikTok Cookbook Trends," dive into the world of viral recipes and food trends. Deconstruct trending dishes, experiment with food hacks and art, and uncover the secrets behind popular TikTok baking trends. Additionally, this chapter explores dietary adaptations, offering vegan, vegetarian, gluten-free, and dairy-free options to cater to various nutritional needs.

Sharing your TikTok culinary creations is crucial to building your presence on the platform. The guide dedicates an entire chapter to this, providing insights into capturing stunning food videos, engaging with the TikTok community, and developing your personal brand as a TikTok food creator.

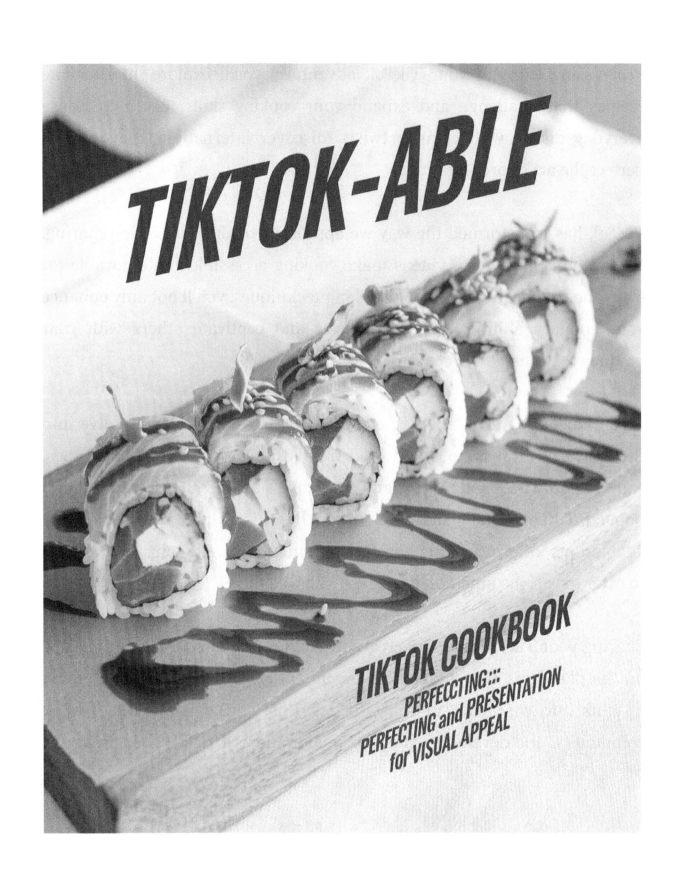

TIKTOK-ABLE

TIKTOK COOKBOOK
PERFECCTING :::
PERFECTING and PRESENTATION
for VISUAL APPEAL

CHAPTER THREE

Exploring TikTok Cookbook Trends

In the fast-moving world of TikTok cooking, trends evolve quickly, capturing the spotlight with each new viral sensation. Chapter 3 of this guide takes you deep into the heart of TikTok cookbook trends, offering an insider's view of the dishes and creative challenges that have taken the platform by storm. Discover the stories behind these trending recipes and the innovative ideas that have captivated millions.

This chapter also highlights the adaptability of TikTok recipes, showcasing how they can be tailored to fit various dietary and lifestyle needs. From vegan and vegetarian options to gluten-free and dairy-free adaptations, you'll see how TikTok's culinary creativity can accommodate a wide range of nutritional preferences and requirements.

Explore the dynamic landscape of TikTok trends and learn how to leverage these insights to inspire your own cooking and content creation. By understanding the mechanics behind viral recipes and embracing diverse dietary adaptations, you'll be well-equipped to stay ahead in the ever-evolving world of TikTok cooking.

Viral Recipes: Behind the Scenes of Trending TikTok Dishes

TikTok is renowned for its ability to turn everyday dishes into viral sensations. This section takes you on a journey behind the scenes of trending TikTok recipes, unraveling their secrets and exploring what makes them so popular. From the famous whipped coffee trend to the mouthwatering feta pasta sensation, you'll discover the stories and techniques behind these viral recipes.

Deconstructing Viral Food Trends and Challenges

TikTok is a hotbed for food trends and challenges that sweep the platform and inspire creators worldwide. In this section, you'll deconstruct the mechanics behind these trends, understanding the key elements that make them captivating and engaging. From the "pancake cereal" trend to the "nature's cereal" sensation, you'll learn how to identify and participate in these trends, adding your own unique twist to the viral recipes.

Trying Your Hand at Food Hacks and Food Art

Food hacks and food art have become iconic on TikTok, showcasing the creativity and ingenuity of creators. This section delves into the world of TikTok-inspired food hacks, offering tips and tricks that will simplify your cooking process and amaze your viewers. From using kitchen gadgets in innovative ways to creating stunning food art installations, you'll be inspired to experiment and push the boundaries of culinary creativity.

Uncovering the Secrets of TikTok Baking Trends

Baking has become a phenomenon on TikTok, with numerous trends captivating the baking community. This section uncovers the secrets behind TikTok baking trends, from the mesmerizing floral cake designs to the gooey stuffed cookies that have taken the platform by storm. Discover the techniques, tools, and tips that will help you achieve bakery-worthy results and join the ranks of TikTok's baking aficionados.

Dietary and Lifestyle Adaptation

One of the strengths of TikTok cooking is its ability to cater to diverse dietary and lifestyle needs. This section explores the adaptations and alternatives available for those following specific dietary preferences or restrictions. Whether you're vegan, vegetarian, gluten-free, or dairy-free,

TikTok offers a wealth of recipes and inspiration to accommodate your nutritional choices.

Vegan and Vegetarian TikTok Recipes

For individuals embracing a plant-based lifestyle, TikTok is a treasure trove of vegan and vegetarian recipes. This section highlights the vibrant and delicious plant-based dishes that have gained popularity on the platform. From creative meat substitutes to innovative flavor combinations, you'll discover how to create satisfying and flavorful meals without animal products.

Gluten-Free and Dairy-Free Alternatives

Living with dietary restrictions such as gluten or dairy intolerance no longer means sacrificing flavor and variety. TikTok offers a plethora of gluten-free and dairy-free alternatives that cater to these needs. In this section, you'll explore recipes that utilize gluten-free flours, dairy-free milks, and innovative ingredient substitutions, ensuring that everyone can enjoy the culinary delights shared on TikTok.

CHAPTER FOUR

From TikTok to Your Kitchen

In today's digital landscape, social media platforms have reshaped numerous aspects of our lives, with the culinary world being a notable example. TikTok, a leading short-form video platform, has emerged as a dynamic force for showcasing innovative and engaging cooking content.

In this chapter, we will delve into the process of bringing TikTok recipes from the screen to your kitchen. You'll learn how to adapt these viral recipes to suit your personal preferences, leverage essential kitchen tools and equipment effectively, and apply strategic tips for recipe testing and modifications. Additionally, we'll explore best practices for sharing your culinary creations, allowing you to build and enhance your personal brand as a TikTok food creator.

Transforming TikTok Recipes into Reality

Adapting TikTok Recipes to Fit Your Taste

One of the exciting aspects of TikTok cooking is the vast array of recipes available. However, not every recipe may align perfectly with your personal preferences or dietary restrictions. That's where adaptation comes into play. When trying out a TikTok recipe, feel free to customize it to suit your taste buds. Experiment with different spices, ingredients, and cooking techniques to add your unique flair to the dish. Don't be afraid to make substitutions or adjustments based on your dietary needs. The beauty of TikTok cooking lies in its versatility, allowing you to make each recipe your own.

Essential Kitchen Tools and Equipment

To successfully bring TikTok recipes to life, it's important to have the right tools and equipment in your kitchen. While many TikTok recipes are designed to be accessible and straightforward, certain kitchen essentials can greatly enhance your cooking experience. Some must-have tools include a sharp chef's knife, a reliable cutting board, measuring spoons and cups, a sturdy blender or food processor, a non-stick skillet, and a baking sheet. These tools will ensure that you can execute a wide range of recipes with ease and precision.

Tips for Recipe Testing and Modifications

Recipe testing is an essential part of the cooking process, especially when trying out TikTok recipes. Here are some tips to help you navigate this stage:

- Read the recipe thoroughly: Before diving into the cooking process, read the recipe carefully from start to finish. Familiarize yourself with the ingredients, measurements, and cooking techniques involved. This will prevent any surprises along the way.

- Test in small batches: When experimenting with a new recipe, it's often a good idea to start with a small batch. This allows you to gauge the flavors and make adjustments before committing to a larger quantity.

- Take notes: Keep a notebook handy during your recipe testing sessions. Jot down any modifications you make, the cooking times, and the results. This will help you refine the recipe and create your version of it.

- Trust your instincts: Don't be afraid to trust your instincts and make changes as you see fit. If a particular ingredient doesn't appeal to you or if you have a substitution in mind, go ahead and try it out. Cooking is a creative process, and your intuition can often lead to delicious outcomes.

CHAPTER FIVE

Sharing Your TikTok Culinary Creations

Capturing Eye-Catching Food Videos

When sharing your culinary creations on TikTok, the visual appeal of your videos is crucial. Consider the following tips to capture eye-catching food videos:

- Lighting: Good lighting is key to showcasing your dishes in the best possible way. Natural light is ideal, so try to position your filming area near a window. If that's not possible, invest in affordable photography lighting kits to ensure well-lit videos.

- Composition: Pay attention to the composition of your shots. Arrange your ingredients and props thoughtfully, and use various angles to add visual interest. Experiment with close-ups, overhead shots, and side angles to create dynamic and engaging footage.

- Presentation: Presentation plays a significant role in making your food videos visually appealing. Take the time to plate your dish attractively, using garnishes, colorful ingredients, and aesthetically pleasing servingware. Attention to detail in the presentation can elevate the overall look of your videos.

- Editing: TikTok provides a range of editing tools and effects to enhance your videos. Experiment with transitions, filters, text overlays, and music to add a professional touch. However, remember to strike a balance and not overuse effects that may distract from the main focus—the food.

Engaging with the TikTok Community

TikTok is not just a platform for sharing videos; it's a vibrant community of creators and viewers. To maximize your engagement and reach on TikTok, consider the following strategies:

- **Engage with Your Audience**: Building a strong connection with your viewers is key to sustaining and growing your presence on TikTok. Take the time to respond to comments, answer questions, and actively engage with your audience. Showing appreciation for their support not only fosters a sense of community but also encourages them to continue following your culinary journey and sharing your content with others. By creating a rapport with your viewers, you enhance their investment in your content and cultivate a loyal fan base.

- **Collaborate with Fellow Creators**: Partnering with other TikTok food creators can significantly expand your reach and introduce you to new audiences. Look for creators whose content resonates with your style or interests and consider proposing a collaboration. Whether it's a joint cooking session, a recipe swap, or a creative challenge, collaborations can offer fresh perspectives and ideas, benefiting both parties and providing your followers with diverse and engaging content.

- **Participate in Challenges and Trends**: TikTok thrives on viral challenges and trends, making them an excellent opportunity for increasing your visibility and engagement. Stay updated on the latest food-related challenges and trends by exploring the "For You" page and trending hashtags. Creating content that aligns with these trends, while adding your unique twist or personal touch, can set your videos apart and attract a wider audience.

- **Utilize Analytics for Growth**: Regularly review TikTok's analytics to gain insights into your content's performance. Analyzing metrics such as views, engagement rates, and audience demographics can help you understand what resonates with your viewers and refine your content strategy. Use these insights to make data-driven decisions, adjust your posting schedule, and experiment with new content formats to optimize your reach and impact.

- **Leverage Cross-Promotion:** Amplify your TikTok presence by cross-promoting your content on other social media platforms. Share snippets of your TikTok videos on Instagram, Facebook, and Twitter to drive traffic to your TikTok profile. Additionally, encourage your followers on these platforms to engage with your TikTok content. Cross-promotion helps broaden your audience and reinforces your brand's presence across multiple channels.

Building Your Personal Brand as a TikTok Food Creator

As you share your culinary creations on TikTok, you have the opportunity to build a personal brand and establish yourself as a food creator. Here are some tips to help you in this process:

- **Consistency**: Building a successful TikTok presence requires regularity. Develop a posting schedule that fits your routine and stick to it. Regular updates signal dedication and keep your audience engaged, helping to build a loyal following over time.

- **Define Your Niche:** Identify what sets you apart in the TikTok food community. Whether it's a focus on a specific cuisine, dietary preferences, or innovative cooking techniques, having a clear niche helps differentiate your content and attracts a dedicated audience interested in your unique perspective.

- **Authenticity**: Authenticity is crucial for connecting with your audience. Let your true self shine through in your videos. Share personal stories, behind-the-scenes insights, and your genuine enthusiasm for cooking. This authenticity builds trust and fosters a deeper connection with viewers.

- **Collaborate with Brands**: As your TikTok presence grows, opportunities for brand collaborations may arise. When partnering with brands, ensure their products align with your values and resonate with your audience. Be transparent about sponsored content while maintaining your authentic voice.

- **Engage with Your Community**: Interact with your viewers by responding to comments, answering questions, and acknowledging their support. Building a rapport with your audience not only fosters a sense of community but also encourages ongoing engagement and word-of-mouth promotion.

- **Explore Cross-Promotion**: Leverage other social media platforms to promote your TikTok content. Share your TikTok videos on Instagram, Facebook, or Twitter to reach a broader audience and drive traffic to your TikTok profile.

- **Analyze and Adapt:** Regularly review your TikTok analytics to understand what content performs best. Pay attention to engagement metrics such as likes, shares, and comments. Use these insights to refine your strategy, experiment with new content formats, and optimize your approach.

- **Participate in Challenges and Trends**: Embrace TikTok's viral challenges and trends to boost visibility and engagement. Create content that aligns with popular food-related trends and add your unique twist to stand out from the crowd.

- **Foster Community Engagement**: Encourage user-generated content by asking your followers to recreate your recipes and tag you in their posts. Feature their creations in your videos to build a sense of community and show appreciation for their participation.

- **Stay Informed and Evolve:** The TikTok landscape is constantly evolving. Stay updated on new features, trends, and best practices to keep your content fresh and relevant. Adapt to changes in the platform to maintain your competitive edge and continue engaging your audience.

CHAPTER SIX

50+ Delicious and Nutritious Recipes with Cooking Tips and Their Nutritional value

The TikTok Cookbook presents an expertly curated collection of the most innovative and delectable recipes that have become culinary sensations on TikTok. Each dish is meticulously designed to be both visually captivating and accessible, ensuring a seamless cooking experience that does not compromise on flavor. In this comprehensive guide, you will explore a diverse array of TikTok-inspired recipes, each accompanied by professional cooking techniques to refine your culinary expertise. Additionally, detailed nutritional information is provided to balance indulgence with health. Embark on an extraordinary culinary journey that merges the latest trends with sophisticated cooking insights, and elevate your kitchen prowess to new heights.

Recipe 1: Baked Feta Pasta

Serves: 4

Preparation time: 10 minutes

Cooking time: 25 minutes

Category: Main Course

Imagine a cozy evening after a long day, the kind where you crave comfort food that feels like a warm hug. Enter the Baked Feta Pasta—a dish that's as comforting as it is trendy. With a touch of Mediterranean flair, this recipe transforms a humble combination of ingredients into a culinary masterpiece. Picture the creamy feta melting into a luscious sauce, mingling with tomatoes and herbs, while the pasta absorbs all those incredible flavors. This is not just dinner; it's a celebration of taste and simplicity.

Ingredients:

- 200g feta cheese
- 400g cherry tomatoes
- 2 cloves garlic, minced
- 300g pasta (penne or your favorite shape)
- 3 tbsp olive oil
- 1 tsp dried oregano
- 1/2 tsp red pepper flakes (optional)
- Fresh basil leaves for garnish
- Salt and pepper to taste

Materials:

- Oven-safe baking dish
- Medium pot
- Colander
- Mixing bowl
- Wooden spoon
- Knife

Procedure:

1. Preheat your oven to 400°F (200°C). Place the block of feta cheese in the center of an oven-safe baking dish.

2. Arrange cherry tomatoes around the feta. Drizzle with olive oil, then sprinkle with minced garlic, oregano, red pepper flakes (if using), salt, and pepper.

3. Roast in the oven for 25-30 minutes, until the tomatoes are blistered and the feta is golden and softened.

4. Meanwhile, cook the pasta according to package instructions until al dente. Drain and set aside.

5. Once the feta and tomatoes are done, use a wooden spoon to gently mash the feta and mix it with the tomatoes, creating a creamy sauce.

6. Toss the cooked pasta into the baking dish, mixing well to coat with the feta-tomato sauce.

7. Garnish with fresh basil leaves and serve immediately, savoring each bite of this delicious, cheesy delight.

Nutritional Value (Per Serving):

- Calories: 450
- Protein: 14g
- Carbohydrates: 60g
- Fat: 18g
- Fiber: 4g

Recipe 2: Whipped Coffee (Dalgona Coffee)

Serves: 2

Preparation time: 5 minutes

Category: Beverage

Picture this: A lazy afternoon, a soft breeze wafting through an open window, and a perfect cup of coffee that feels like a cloud in your mug. Whipped Coffee, or Dalgona Coffee, became an internet sensation for good reason. It's not just a drink; it's a moment of indulgence and creativity. With its airy, frothy texture and rich, creamy flavor, this beverage is as delightful to make as it is to enjoy. As you whip your coffee to perfection, you're crafting a dreamy experience that turns a regular cup of joe into a luxurious treat.

Ingredients:

- 2 tbsp instant coffee
- 2 tbsp granulated sugar
- 2 tbsp hot water
- 1 cup milk (whole, almond, or your preferred variety)
- Ice cubes (optional)

Materials:

- Mixing bowl
- Electric mixer or whisk
- Measuring spoons
- Cup
- Spoon

Procedure:

1. In a mixing bowl, combine instant coffee, granulated sugar, and hot water.
2. Using an electric mixer or a whisk, beat the mixture on high speed for about 3-5 minutes, or until it becomes thick, creamy, and forms stiff peaks.
3. Pour milk into a cup, adding ice cubes if you like your coffee cold.
4. Spoon the whipped coffee mixture over the milk, creating a beautiful, frothy layer on top.
5. Stir before sipping to blend the creamy coffee with the milk, and enjoy the velvety smooth texture and rich flavor of your homemade Dalgona Coffee.

Nutritional Value (Per Serving):

- Calories: 120
- Protein: 3g
- Carbohydrates: 24g
- Fat: 1g
- Fiber: 0g

Recipe 3: Cloud Bread

Makes: 6-8 cloud breads

Preparation time: 15 minutes

Cooking time: 25 minutes

Category: Snack

Imagine a whimsical creation that defies the laws of baking—a bread so light and airy it feels like biting into a fluffy cloud. Cloud Bread, with its ethereal texture and subtly sweet flavor, is not just a treat but an enchanting experience. Originating from the digital world, this recipe has taken the culinary realm by storm, offering a unique and delightful twist on traditional bread. As you whip and bake, you'll transform simple ingredients into a fluffy, cloud-like delight that promises to elevate your snacking game to celestial heights.

Ingredients:

- 3 large egg whites
- 1/4 tsp cream of tartar
- 1/4 cup granulated sugar
- 2 tbsp cornstarch
- 1/2 tsp vanilla extract (optional)

Materials:

- Mixing bowl
- Electric mixer or whisk
- Baking sheet
- Parchment paper
- Spatula

Procedure:

1. Preheat your oven to 300°F (150°C) and line a baking sheet with parchment paper.

2. In a mixing bowl, beat the egg whites and cream of tartar with an electric mixer or whisk until stiff peaks form.

3. Gradually add granulated sugar and continue to beat until the mixture is glossy and holds stiff peaks.

4. Gently fold in cornstarch and vanilla extract (if using) until fully incorporated, being careful not to deflate the mixture.

5. Spoon the mixture onto the prepared baking sheet, shaping it into a round loaf or individual mounds.

6. Bake for 25-30 minutes, or until the cloud bread is golden and firm to the touch.

7. Allow it to cool completely before slicing and savoring your light, airy creation.

Nutritional Value (Per Serving, based on 4 servings):

- Calories: 50
- Protein: 1g
- Carbohydrates: 12g
- Fat: 0g
- Fiber: 0g

Recipe 4: Baked Oats

Serves: 2

Preparation time: 10 minutes

Cooking time: 25 minutes

Category: Breakfast

Start your day with a breakfast that feels like a warm hug—Baked Oats. This recipe transforms humble oats into a cozy, baked delight that's perfect for those chilly mornings or a comforting start to any day. Imagine your kitchen filled with the aroma of baked cinnamon and vanilla as you prepare this wholesome dish. Each spoonful is a blend of soft, comforting oats with a hint of sweetness and warmth. Baked Oats are not just a meal; they're a morning ritual that combines nourishment with a touch of indulgence.

Ingredients:

- 1 cup rolled oats
- 1/2 cup milk (dairy or plant-based)
- 1/4 cup honey or maple syrup
- 1/4 cup Greek yogurt or applesauce
- 1/2 tsp vanilla extract
- 1/2 tsp baking powder
- 1/2 tsp ground cinnamon
- Pinch of salt
- Optional toppings: fresh fruit, nuts, chocolate chips, or seeds

Materials:

- Mixing bowl
- Spoon or spatula
- Baking dish (8x8 inches)
- Oven

Procedure:

1. Preheat your oven to 350°F (175°C) and lightly grease a baking dish.
2. In a mixing bowl, combine rolled oats, milk, honey (or maple syrup), Greek yogurt (or applesauce), vanilla extract, baking powder, ground cinnamon, and a pinch of salt. Stir until well mixed.

3. Pour the oat mixture into the prepared baking dish and spread it evenly.

4. Add any optional toppings you like, such as fresh fruit, nuts, or chocolate chips.

5. Bake for 30-35 minutes, or until the top is golden and the oats are set.

6. Allow it to cool slightly before serving, and enjoy a hearty, satisfying breakfast.

Nutritional Value (Per Serving, based on 4 servings):

- Calories: 220
- Protein: 8g
- Carbohydrates: 35g
- Fat: 6g
- Fiber: 4g

Recipe 5: Tortilla Wrap Hack

Serves: 1

Preparation time: 5 minutes

Category: Lunch/Dinner

Imagine a lunchtime revolution with the Tortilla Wrap Hack—a culinary trick that turns an ordinary tortilla into a deliciously versatile meal. This clever technique will have you saying goodbye to the mundane and hello to a world of flavor-packed possibilities. Picture yourself effortlessly layering ingredients into a tortilla, transforming it into a neat, easy-to-eat wrap that's perfect for any meal. Whether you're at home or on the go, this hack brings a touch of creativity and convenience to your everyday eating routine.

Ingredients:

- 1 large tortilla (flour or whole wheat)
- 2-3 tablespoons of your favorite spread (hummus, guacamole, or cream cheese)
- 1/2 cup cooked protein (chicken, tofu, or beans)
- 1/2 cup fresh vegetables (lettuce, bell peppers, cucumbers, or tomatoes)
- 1/4 cup shredded cheese (cheddar, mozzarella, or feta)
- Optional: additional seasonings or sauces (salsa, hot sauce, or a drizzle of olive oil)

Materials:

- Knife or scissors
- Cutting board
- Spatula or spoon
- Plate

Procedure:

1. Place the tortilla flat on a cutting board. Using a knife or scissors, make a cut from the center of the tortilla to the edge, creating a four-section shape.
2. Begin layering your spread of choice onto one section of the tortilla.
3. On the adjacent section, add your cooked protein and spread it out evenly.

4. In the next section, layer your fresh vegetables and cheese.

5. Fold the tortilla into a wrap by starting from the cut edge and folding over each section in a clockwise or counterclockwise direction, creating a neat, folded wrap.

6. Heat a non-stick skillet over medium heat and place the wrap seam-side down. Cook for 2-3 minutes on each side, or until the tortilla is golden and the cheese is melted.

7. Slice in half if desired, and enjoy a convenient, flavorful meal.

Nutritional Value (Per Serving, based on 1 wrap):

- Calories: 350
- Protein: 20g
- Carbohydrates: 40g
- Fat: 15g
- Fiber: 6g

Recipe 6: Pancake Cereal

Serves: 2

Preparation time: 10 minutes

Cooking time: 10 minutes

Category: Breakfast

Step into a breakfast fantasy with Pancake Cereal—a delightful twist on your morning routine that's as fun to make as it is to eat. Imagine a bowl brimming with tiny, fluffy pancakes swimming in syrup, each bite a burst of pure breakfast bliss. This whimsical recipe transforms the classic pancake into a bite-sized treat, perfect for a quick, satisfying start to your day. With just a splash of milk and a sprinkle of fresh fruit, Pancake Cereal turns an ordinary breakfast into an extraordinary experience.

Ingredients:

- 1 cup all-purpose flour
- 1 tablespoon sugar
- 1 teaspoon baking powder
- 1/2 teaspoon baking soda
- 1/4 teaspoon salt
- 3/4 cup buttermilk
- 1/4 cup milk
- 1 large egg
- 2 tablespoons melted butter
- Optional toppings: maple syrup, fresh berries, sliced bananas

Materials:

- Mixing bowls
- Whisk
- Frying pan or griddle
- Small round cookie cutter or bottle for mini pancakes
- Ladle or small spoon

Procedure:

1. In a mixing bowl, whisk together the flour, sugar, baking powder, baking soda, and salt.
2. In another bowl, combine the buttermilk, milk, egg, and melted butter. Mix until well combined.
3. Pour the wet ingredients into the dry ingredients and gently stir until just combined. Avoid overmixing—small lumps are okay.

4. Heat a non-stick frying pan or griddle over medium heat and lightly grease it.

5. Using a small round cookie cutter or bottle, pour small amounts of batter onto the pan to create mini pancakes. Cook for about 1-2 minutes per side, or until golden brown and bubbles appear on the surface.

6. Once cooked, transfer the mini pancakes to a plate.

7. Serve the pancake cereal in a bowl, drizzle with maple syrup, and top with fresh berries or sliced bananas.

Nutritional Value (Per Serving, based on 1 cup of mini pancakes without toppings):

- Calories: 350
- Protein: 8g
- Carbohydrates: 50g
- Fat: 14g
- Fiber: 2g

Recipe 7: Cloud Bread Ice Cream Sandwiches

Makes: 4 ice cream sandwiches

Preparation time: 15 minutes

Cooking time: 25 minutes

Category: Dessert

Imagine biting into a dessert that feels like a fluffy cloud but tastes like sweet indulgence. Cloud Bread Ice Cream Sandwiches elevate this whimsical treat into a new realm of deliciousness. With its light, airy texture, cloud bread provides the perfect canvas for creamy, cool ice cream. Picture this: a warm, sunny afternoon, a gentle breeze, and you holding a cloud-like sandwich filled with your favorite ice cream flavor. It's a dreamy treat that turns any day into a celebration.

Ingredients:

For the Cloud Bread:

- 3 large egg whites
- 1/2 cup granulated sugar
- 1/2 teaspoon vanilla extract
- 1/4 teaspoon cream of tartar
- 1/4 cup cornstarch

For the Ice Cream Filling:

- 1 pint of your favorite ice cream (softened for easier spreading)

Materials:

- Mixing bowls
- Electric mixer
- Baking sheet
- Parchment paper
- Spatula
- Ice cream scoop

Procedure:

1. Preheat your oven to 300°F (150°C). Line a baking sheet with parchment paper.

2. In a clean mixing bowl, use an electric mixer to beat the egg whites on medium speed until foamy. Add the cream of tartar and continue to beat until soft peaks form.

3. Gradually add the granulated sugar while beating on high speed until stiff peaks form and the mixture is glossy.

4. Gently fold in the vanilla extract and cornstarch until well combined.

5. Spoon dollops of the meringue mixture onto the prepared baking sheet, spreading each dollop into a round shape about 3 inches in diameter. You can use the back of a spoon to shape them.

6. Bake for 25-30 minutes, or until the cloud bread is crisp on the outside and slightly soft on the inside. Let it cool completely on a wire rack.

7. Once cooled, spread a generous amount of softened ice cream onto the flat side of one cloud bread round. Top with another round to form a sandwich.

8. Repeat with remaining cloud bread and ice cream.

Nutritional Value (Per Serving, based on 1 sandwich, with vanilla ice cream):

- Calories: 350
- Protein: 4g
- Carbohydrates: 36g
- Fat: 20g
- Fiber: 1g

Recipe 8: Dalgona Matcha Latte

Serves: 1

Preparation time: 5 minutes

Category: Beverage

Step into the world of vibrant green and frothy indulgence with the Dalgona Matcha Latte—a modern twist on the classic whipped coffee trend. This matcha latte blends the smooth, earthy flavors of matcha with a cloud-like, whipped topping that turns a simple drink into an Instagram-worthy masterpiece. Imagine savoring this creamy, frothy beverage as you unwind on a cozy afternoon or as a pick-me-up during a busy day. It's the perfect way to enjoy a moment of zen and a splash of green goodness.

Ingredients:

- For the Whipped Matcha Topping:
    - 2 tablespoons matcha powder
    - 2 tablespoons granulated sugar
    - 1 tablespoon hot water
- For the Latte:
    - 1 cup milk (dairy or plant-based)
    - 1 teaspoon honey or maple syrup (optional, for sweetness)
    - Ice cubes (optional)

Materials:

- Mixing bowl
- Electric mixer or whisk
- Measuring spoons
- Glass or mug
- Spoon

Procedure:

1. In a mixing bowl, combine the matcha powder, granulated sugar, and hot water.
2. Using an electric mixer or whisk, beat the mixture until it becomes frothy and thickened to a whipped consistency. This should take about 2-3 minutes.
3. In a separate glass or mug, heat the milk until warm (or cold if you prefer an iced latte). If using a sweetener, stir it into the milk.
4. If desired, add ice cubes to the glass before pouring in the milk.

5. Spoon the whipped matcha topping generously over the milk. Use a spoon or straw to mix it together or enjoy it as is.

6. Sip and enjoy the blend of creamy, frothy matcha goodness.

Nutritional Value (Per Serving, without added sweetener):

- Calories: 180
- Protein: 7g
- Carbohydrates: 18g
- Fat: 7g
- Fiber: 1g

Recipe 9: Mini Pesto Zucchini Noodles

Serves: 2

Preparation time: 10 minutes

Cooking time: 5 minutes

Category: Appetizer/Snack

Get ready to elevate your snacking game with these Mini Pesto Zucchini Noodles—where vibrant, fresh flavors meet a touch of sophistication. Imagine a sunlit kitchen, the scent of basil and garlic filling the air as you prepare these delightful, bite-sized noodles. Perfect for a light appetizer or a health-conscious snack, these zucchini noodles bring together the creamy richness of pesto and the crisp, refreshing crunch of fresh zucchini. It's like having a gourmet experience at your fingertips.

Ingredients:

- 2 medium zucchinis
- 1/4 cup homemade or store-bought pesto sauce
- 1 tablespoon olive oil
- 1 tablespoon pine nuts (optional, for garnish)
- 2 tablespoons grated Parmesan cheese (optional, for garnish)
- Salt and pepper to taste

Materials:

- Spiralizer or vegetable peeler
- Large bowl
- Small skillet (if toasting pine nuts)
- Tongs or fork

Procedure:

1. Spiralize the zucchinis into thin noodles using a spiralizer or vegetable peeler. Place the noodles in a large bowl.

2. In a small skillet, heat the olive oil over medium heat. If using pine nuts, add them to the skillet and toast until golden brown, about 2-3 minutes. Remove from heat and set aside.

3. Toss the zucchini noodles with the pesto sauce until they are evenly coated. Add salt and pepper to taste.

4. Transfer the noodles to a serving plate or bowl.

5. Garnish with toasted pine nuts and grated Parmesan cheese if desired.

6. Serve immediately and enjoy a fresh, flavorful bite.

Nutritional Value (Per Serving, without added garnishes):

- Calories: 110
- Protein: 3g
- Carbohydrates: 8g
- Fat: 9g
- Fiber: 2g

Recipe 10: TikTok Ramen Hack

Serves: 1

Preparation time: 5 minutes

Cooking time: 10 minutes

Category: Main Course

Imagine a bowl of ramen that's both comforting and inventive, elevating your typical instant noodle experience to a gourmet delight. This TikTok Ramen Hack takes the beloved instant ramen and gives it a flavorful, upscale twist. Picture yourself cozying up on a chilly evening, savoring each slurp of noodles enriched with savory broth and added extras. With this recipe, you're not just making ramen—you're crafting a bowl of noodle perfection that's as satisfying as it is innovative.

Ingredients:

- 1 package instant ramen noodles
- 2 cups chicken or vegetable broth
- 1 tablespoon soy sauce
- 1 teaspoon sesame oil
- 1 clove garlic, minced
- 1/2 teaspoon ginger, minced
- 1/2 cup frozen peas
- 1/2 cup sliced mushrooms
- 1 green onion, sliced
- 1 large egg
- Optional toppings: cooked chicken, bamboo shoots, spinach, nori, or sriracha

Materials:

- Medium saucepan
- Small skillet (for cooking egg)
- Whisk
- Bowl

Procedure:

1. In a medium saucepan, bring the chicken or vegetable broth to a simmer over medium heat. Add soy sauce, sesame oil, garlic, and ginger. Stir well and let it simmer for about 3 minutes to allow the flavors to meld.

2. Add the instant ramen noodles to the broth and cook according to the package instructions, usually about 3 minutes.

3. In a small skillet, cook the egg to your preference—soft-boiled, poached, or even scrambled. For a soft-boiled egg, bring water to a boil, gently add the egg, and cook for 6 minutes. Transfer to ice water and peel.

4. Add the frozen peas and sliced mushrooms to the broth during the last minute of cooking, allowing them to heat through.

5. Ladle the ramen into a bowl and top with sliced green onions and your choice of optional toppings.

6. Gently place the cooked egg on top, and add a dash of sriracha if desired for a spicy kick.

7. Stir and enjoy the enhanced flavors of your upgraded ramen.

Nutritional Value (Per Serving, without additional toppings):

- Calories: 290
- Protein: 12g
- Carbohydrates: 30g
- Fat: 13g
- Fiber: 3g

Recipe 11: Baked Feta Pasta with Shrimp

Serves: 4

Preparation time: 10 minutes

Cooking time: 35 minutes

Category: Main Course

Elevate your pasta game with a recipe that has taken social media by storm. The Baked Feta Pasta with Shrimp combines the creamy decadence of baked feta with succulent shrimp for a dish that's as delightful to eat as it is to prepare. Imagine a cozy evening, the aroma of melting cheese wafting through the kitchen, and a steaming bowl of pasta that perfectly balances richness and freshness. This recipe transforms a viral sensation into a gourmet experience, making your meal a highlight of the week.

Ingredients:

- 1 block of feta cheese (200g)
- 2 cups cherry tomatoes, halved
- 1/4 cup extra-virgin olive oil
- 2 cloves garlic, minced
- 1 teaspoon dried oregano
- 1/2 teaspoon dried basil
- 1/4 teaspoon red pepper flakes (optional)
- 8 ounces pasta (penne or rigatoni work well)
- 1 pound shrimp, peeled and deveined
- Salt and pepper to taste
- Fresh basil, chopped (for garnish)
- Grated Parmesan cheese (for serving, optional)

Materials:

- Oven-safe baking dish
- Medium pot
- Large skillet
- Mixing bowl
- Wooden spoon or spatula

Procedure:

1. Preheat your oven to 400°F (200°C). In an oven-safe baking dish, place the block of feta cheese in the center. Arrange cherry tomatoes around the feta.

2. Drizzle the feta and tomatoes with olive oil, and sprinkle minced garlic, dried oregano, dried basil, and red pepper flakes (if using) over the top. Season with salt and pepper.

3. Bake in the preheated oven for 20-25 minutes, until the feta is soft and the tomatoes are bursting.

4. While the feta and tomatoes are baking, cook the pasta according to package instructions until al dente. Drain and set aside.

5. In a large skillet over medium heat, add a drizzle of olive oil. Season the shrimp with salt and pepper, and cook for 2-3 minutes per side, until pink and opaque. Remove from the skillet and set aside.

6. Once the feta and tomatoes are baked, use a fork to mash the feta and tomatoes together, creating a creamy sauce. Mix in the cooked pasta until well coated.

7. Gently fold in the cooked shrimp, and garnish with fresh chopped basil.

8. Serve immediately, with grated Parmesan cheese if desired.

Nutritional Value (Per Serving):

- Calories: 470
- Protein: 25g
- Carbohydrates: 50g
- Fat: 20g
- Fiber: 4g

Recipe 12: Teriyaki Chicken Skewers

Serves: 4

Preparation time: 15 minutes

Cooking time: 10 minutes

Category: Main Course

Transport yourself to a bustling street market with these Teriyaki Chicken Skewers, where the sweet and savory aroma of teriyaki sauce fills the air. Picture a vibrant evening, a grill sizzling with tender chicken skewers, and the anticipation of a mouthwatering meal that brings together bold flavors and simple ingredients. This recipe infuses traditional Japanese flavors into a convenient and delicious skewer format, making it perfect for any gathering or a cozy night in.

Ingredients:

- 1 pound boneless, skinless chicken breasts or thighs, cut into bite-sized pieces
- 1/2 cup teriyaki sauce
- 2 tablespoons soy sauce
- 2 tablespoons honey
- 1 tablespoon rice vinegar
- 1 tablespoon sesame oil
- 2 cloves garlic, minced
- 1 teaspoon freshly grated ginger
- 1 tablespoon vegetable oil (for grilling)
- Sesame seeds (for garnish)
- Green onions, chopped (for garnish)

Materials:

- Skewers (wooden or metal)
- Mixing bowl
- Grill or grill pan
- Small saucepan
- Brush or spoon (for basting)

Procedure:

1. **Marinate the Chicken:** In a mixing bowl, combine teriyaki sauce, soy sauce, honey, rice vinegar, sesame oil, minced garlic, and grated ginger. Stir well. Add the chicken pieces to the marinade, ensuring

they are well-coated. Cover and refrigerate for at least 30 minutes, or up to 2 hours for more flavor.

2. **Prepare the Skewers:** If using wooden skewers, soak them in water for 30 minutes before grilling to prevent burning. Thread the marinated chicken pieces onto the skewers.

3. **Preheat the Grill:** Heat your grill or grill pan to medium-high heat. Lightly oil the grill grates with a paper towel dipped in vegetable oil.

4. **Grill the Skewers:** Place the chicken skewers on the grill and cook for 4-5 minutes per side, or until the chicken is fully cooked and has a nice char. Baste the chicken with leftover marinade during grilling for extra flavor.

5. **Garnish and Serve:** Once cooked, remove the skewers from the grill. Sprinkle with sesame seeds and chopped green onions for added texture and freshness.

6. **Enjoy:** Serve the Teriyaki Chicken Skewers with steamed rice or a fresh vegetable salad for a complete meal.

Nutritional Value (Per Serving, 2 skewers):

- Calories: 230
- Protein: 25g
- Carbohydrates: 10g
- Fat: 10g
- Fiber: 1g

Recipe 13: Caprese Stuffed Portobello Mushrooms

Serves: 4

Preparation time: 15 minutes

Cooking time: 20 minutes

Category: Appetizer

Imagine a warm, inviting kitchen filled with the rich aroma of roasted mushrooms mingling with the freshness of basil and the creamy delight of mozzarella. These Caprese Stuffed Portobello Mushrooms turn a classic Caprese salad into an elegant, savory appetizer that's perfect for a cozy dinner party or a delightful weeknight treat. With each bite, you'll experience the harmony of flavors and textures, a testament to the beauty of simple, fresh ingredients.

Ingredients:

- 4 large Portobello mushrooms
- 1 cup cherry tomatoes, halved
- 1 cup fresh mozzarella balls (or shredded mozzarella)
- 1/4 cup fresh basil leaves, chopped
- 2 tablespoons balsamic glaze
- 2 tablespoons olive oil
- 1 clove garlic, minced
- Salt and pepper to taste

Materials:

- Baking sheet
- Oven
- Spoon (for scooping)
- Small bowl
- Basting brush

Procedure:

1. **Preheat the Oven:** Set your oven to 375°F (190°C) and line a baking sheet with parchment paper or lightly grease it.
2. **Prepare the Mushrooms:** Gently remove the stems from the Portobello mushrooms and scoop out the gills using a spoon to create space for the stuffing. Brush the mushroom caps with olive oil and season with salt and pepper.

3. **Mix the Filling:** In a small bowl, combine cherry tomatoes, mozzarella, chopped basil, and minced garlic. Drizzle with a bit of olive oil and season with salt and pepper to taste.

4. **Stuff the Mushrooms:** Place the mushroom caps on the baking sheet, gill side up. Spoon the tomato and mozzarella mixture generously into each mushroom cap.

5. **Bake:** Place the baking sheet in the oven and bake for 15-20 minutes, or until the mushrooms are tender and the cheese is melted and bubbly.

6. **Garnish and Serve:** Remove the mushrooms from the oven and drizzle with balsamic glaze. Garnish with additional fresh basil if desired.

7. **Enjoy:** Serve warm as an appetizer or a light main course, and savor the blend of rich, umami flavors with the freshness of basil and the sweetness of balsamic glaze.

Nutritional Value (Per Serving, 2 stuffed mushrooms):

- Calories: 150
- Protcin: 8g
- Carbohydrates: 12g
- Fat: 8g
- Fiber: 2g

Recipe 14: Grilled Honey Lime Chicken

Serves: 4

Preparation time: 10 minutes

Marinating time: 30 minutes

Cooking time: 10 minutes

Category: Main Course

Picture yourself on a summer evening, the grill sizzling with the tantalizing aroma of honey-lime glazed chicken. This Grilled Honey Lime Chicken brings together the sweetness of honey and the zesty brightness of lime in a mouthwatering marinade that caramelizes beautifully on the grill. Each bite is a harmonious blend of flavors, perfect for a casual family dinner or an outdoor barbecue with friends.

Ingredients:

- 4 boneless, skinless chicken breasts
- 1/4 cup honey
- 1/4 cup freshly squeezed lime juice (about 2 limes)
- 2 tablespoons olive oil
- 3 cloves garlic, minced
- 1 teaspoon ground cumin
- 1/2 teaspoon paprika
- 1/2 teaspoon salt
- 1/4 teaspoon black pepper
- Fresh cilantro for garnish (optional)

Materials:

- Mixing bowl
- Whisk
- Grill or grill pan
- Tongs
- Basting brush

Procedure:

1. **Prepare the Marinade:** In a mixing bowl, whisk together honey, lime juice, olive oil, minced garlic, cumin, paprika, salt, and pepper until well combined.
2. **Marinate the Chicken:** Place the chicken breasts in a resealable plastic bag or shallow dish. Pour the marinade over the chicken, ensuring it's evenly coated. Seal the bag or cover the dish and

refrigerate for at least 30 minutes, or up to 2 hours for a deeper flavor.

3. **Preheat the Grill:** Preheat your grill to medium-high heat. If using a grill pan, heat it over medium-high heat on the stove.

4. **Grill the Chicken:** Remove the chicken from the marinade and discard the excess marinade. Place the chicken breasts on the grill or grill pan. Cook for 6-7 minutes on each side, or until the chicken reaches an internal temperature of 165°F (74°C) and has nice grill marks.

5. **Baste and Finish:** During the last few minutes of grilling, brush the chicken with a little more marinade to enhance the flavor and achieve a glossy finish.

6. **Garnish and Serve:** Remove the chicken from the grill and let it rest for a few minutes. Garnish with fresh cilantro if desired and serve with your favorite sides.

Nutritional Value (Per Serving, 1 chicken breast):

- Calories: 230
- Protein: 30g
- Carbohydrates: 14g
- Fat: 8g
- Fiber: 1g

Recipe 15: Vegetable Stir-Fry

Serves: 4

Preparation time: 15 minutes

Cooking time: 10 minutes

Category: Main Course

Imagine a vibrant, colorful medley of fresh vegetables sizzling in a hot pan, releasing their natural juices and mingling with a savory sauce. This Vegetable Stir-Fry is a celebration of crisp textures and bold flavors that come together in a matter of minutes. Perfect for busy weeknights or a quick lunch, this dish showcases how simple ingredients can transform into a nutritious and satisfying meal.

Ingredients:

- 1 tablespoon vegetable oil
- 1 red bell pepper, sliced
- 1 yellow bell pepper, sliced
- 1 cup broccoli florets
- 1 cup snap peas
- 1 carrot, sliced thinly
- 1/2 cup mushrooms, sliced
- 3 cloves garlic, minced
- 1 tablespoon fresh ginger, minced
- 3 tablespoons soy sauce
- 2 tablespoons hoisin sauce
- 1 tablespoon rice vinegar
- 1 teaspoon sesame oil
- 1 tablespoon cornstarch mixed with 2 tablespoons water (for thickening, optional)
- Cooked rice or noodles for serving
- Sesame seeds for garnish (optional)

Materials:

- Wok or large skillet
- Spatula or wooden spoon
- Measuring spoons
- Small bowl (for sauce mixture)

Procedure:

1. **Prepare the Sauce:** In a small bowl, mix together soy sauce, hoisin sauce, rice vinegar, and sesame oil. Set aside.

2. **Heat the Pan:** Heat vegetable oil in a wok or large skillet over medium-high heat until hot.

3. **Stir-Fry the Vegetables:** Add garlic and ginger to the pan, sautéing for about 30 seconds until fragrant. Add the bell peppers, broccoli, snap peas, carrot, and mushrooms. Stir-fry for 5-7 minutes, or until the vegetables are crisp-tender.

4. **Add the Sauce:** Pour the sauce over the vegetables, tossing to coat evenly. If desired, add the cornstarch mixture to thicken the sauce, stirring continuously until the sauce has thickened to your liking.

5. **Serve:** Remove from heat and serve immediately over cooked rice or noodles. Garnish with sesame seeds if desired.

Nutritional Value (Per Serving, excluding rice or noodles):

-   Calories: 150
-   Protein: 4g
-   Carbohydrates: 23g
-   Fat: 6g
-   Fiber: 4g

Recipe 16: Quinoa Salad with Roasted Vegetables

Serves: 4

Preparation time: 15 minutes

Cooking time: 25 minutes

Category: Salad

Picture a vibrant bowl brimming with roasted vegetables and fluffy quinoa, all tossed together with a zesty dressing. This Quinoa Salad with Roasted Vegetables is not just a meal; it's an experience of crunchy textures and hearty flavors in every bite. It's the kind of dish that effortlessly transitions from a comforting dinner to a refreshing lunch the next day, making it a versatile addition to your culinary repertoire.

Ingredients:

- 1 cup quinoa
- 2 cups water or vegetable broth
- 1 red bell pepper, diced
- 1 zucchini, diced
- 1 cup cherry tomatoes, halved
- 1 red onion, diced
- 2 tablespoons olive oil
- 1 teaspoon dried oregano
- 1/2 teaspoon smoked paprika
- Salt and pepper to taste
- 1/4 cup crumbled feta cheese (optional)
- 1/4 cup fresh basil, chopped

For the Dressing:

- 3 tablespoons olive oil
- 2 tablespoons balsamic vinegar
- 1 tablespoon Dijon mustard
- 1 teaspoon honey
- 1 garlic clove, minced
- Salt and pepper to taste

Materials:

- Medium saucepan
- Baking sheet
- Large bowl

- Whisk

Procedure:

1. **Cook the Quinoa:** Rinse quinoa under cold water. In a medium saucepan, bring water or vegetable broth to a boil. Add quinoa, reduce heat to low, cover, and simmer for 15 minutes, or until quinoa is tender and liquid is absorbed. Fluff with a fork and let cool.
2. **Roast the Vegetables:** Preheat your oven to 425°F (220°C). On a baking sheet, toss bell pepper, zucchini, cherry tomatoes, and red onion with olive oil, oregano, smoked paprika, salt, and pepper. Roast for 20-25 minutes, or until vegetables are tender and lightly caramelized.
3. **Prepare the Dressing:** In a small bowl, whisk together olive oil, balsamic vinegar, Dijon mustard, honey, garlic, salt, and pepper until well combined.
4. **Assemble the Salad:** In a large bowl, combine cooked quinoa, roasted vegetables, and crumbled feta cheese if using. Drizzle with the dressing and toss to coat evenly.
5. **Garnish and Serve:** Sprinkle with fresh basil before serving. Enjoy warm or chilled.

Nutritional Value (Per Serving, assuming 4 servings):

- Calories: 290
- Protein: 8g
- Carbohydrates: 38g
- Fat: 12g
- Fiber: 6g

Recipe 17: One-Pot Mexican Quinoa

Serves: 4

Preparation time: 10 minutes

Cooking time: 25 minutes

Category: Main Course

Imagine a one-pot wonder that combines the vibrant flavors of Mexico with the hearty, nutritious goodness of quinoa. This One-Pot Mexican Quinoa is the ultimate comfort food—spicy, savory, and incredibly satisfying. Whether you're winding down after a busy day or prepping for a family feast, this dish delivers a burst of flavor and a colorful presentation that will make every bite an adventure.

Ingredients:

- 1 cup quinoa
- 1 tablespoon olive oil
- 1 small onion, diced
- 2 cloves garlic, minced
- 1 red bell pepper, diced
- 1 green bell pepper, diced
- 1 cup corn kernels (fresh, frozen, or canned)
- 1 can (15 oz) black beans, drained and rinsed
- 1 can (15 oz) diced tomatoes with green chilies
- 1 teaspoon ground cumin
- 1 teaspoon smoked paprika
- 1/2 teaspoon chili powder
- Salt and pepper to taste
- 2 cups vegetable broth
- 1/2 cup chopped fresh cilantro
- 1 lime, cut into wedges
- Optional toppings: shredded cheese, avocado slices, sour cream

Materials:

- Large pot or Dutch oven
- Wooden spoon
- Measuring cups and spoons

Procedure:

1. **Sauté the Aromatics:** In a large pot or Dutch oven, heat olive oil over medium heat. Add diced onion and cook until translucent, about 5 minutes. Stir in garlic and cook for another minute until fragrant.

2. **Cook the Vegetables:** Add red and green bell peppers to the pot. Cook, stirring occasionally, until they start to soften, about 5 minutes.

3. **Combine the Ingredients:** Stir in corn, black beans, diced tomatoes with green chilies, cumin, smoked paprika, chili powder, salt, and pepper. Cook for a few minutes to blend the flavors.

4. **Add the Quinoa:** Rinse quinoa under cold water and add it to the pot. Pour in vegetable broth and bring to a boil.

5. **Simmer and Cook:** Reduce heat to low, cover, and let it simmer for 15-20 minutes, or until the quinoa is cooked and the liquid is absorbed. Fluff with a fork and stir in fresh cilantro.

6. **Serve and Garnish:** Serve hot, garnished with lime wedges and optional toppings like shredded cheese, avocado slices, and sour cream.

Nutritional Value (Per Serving, assuming 4 servings):

- Calories: 350
- Protein: 12g
- Carbohydrates: 50g
- Fat: 10g
- Fiber: 8g

Recipe 18: Baked Parmesan Zucchini Fries

Serves: 4

Preparation time: 15 minutes

Cooking time: 20 minutes

Category: Appetizer

Craving a crispy, savory snack that won't derail your healthy eating goals? These Baked Parmesan Zucchini Fries are just what you need. Picture a crunchy, golden exterior giving way to tender, flavorful zucchini inside—perfect for snacking, dipping, or as a side to your favorite meal. This recipe is a delicious twist on traditional fries, offering all the satisfaction with a fraction of the calories. Plus, they're baked to crispy perfection without the mess of frying.

Ingredients:

- 3 medium zucchinis
- 1 cup panko breadcrumbs
- 1/2 cup grated Parmesan cheese
- 1/2 teaspoon garlic powder
- 1/2 teaspoon onion powder
- 1/2 teaspoon dried oregano
- 1/2 teaspoon paprika
- 1/4 teaspoon black pepper
- 2 large eggs

Cooking spray

- Optional: marinara sauce or ranch dressing for dipping

Materials:

- Baking sheet
- Wire rack (optional)
- Three shallow bowls
- Knife
- Cutting board
- Whisk

Procedure:

1. Prep the Zucchini: Preheat your oven to 425°F (220°C). Line a baking sheet with parchment paper or lightly grease it. Slice the zucchinis into thin, fry-shaped strips, about 1/4-inch thick.

2. Prepare the Coating: In one shallow bowl, whisk the eggs. In a second shallow bowl, combine panko breadcrumbs, grated Parmesan, garlic powder, onion powder, oregano, paprika, and black pepper.

3. Coat the Zucchini: Dip each zucchini strip into the egg mixture, allowing excess to drip off, then coat thoroughly with the breadcrumb mixture. Place the coated strips on the prepared baking sheet. For extra crispiness, place the coated zucchini on a wire rack set over the baking sheet.

4. Bake: Lightly spray the zucchini fries with cooking spray. Bake in the preheated oven for 20-25 minutes, or until they are golden brown and crispy, turning halfway through the baking time.

5. Serve: Allow the zucchini fries to cool slightly before serving. Enjoy with marinara sauce or ranch dressing if desired.

Nutritional Value (Per Serving, assuming 4 servings):

- Calories: 150
- Protein: 7g
- Carbohydrates: 15g
- Fat: 7g
- Fiber: 3g

Recipe 19: Thai Coconut Curry Soup

Serves: 4

Preparation time: 10 minutes

Cooking time: 25 minutes

Category: Soup

Picture a steaming bowl of Thai Coconut Curry Soup, brimming with vibrant flavors and a rich, aromatic broth. This recipe brings the essence of Thai street food to your kitchen, transforming simple ingredients into a soul-warming, exotic delight. Imagine a cool evening with a bowl of this creamy, spicy soup, the gentle heat of the curry warming you from the inside out. It's a culinary journey to Thailand with every spoonful, perfect for a cozy dinner or impressing guests with something truly special.

Ingredients:

- 1 tablespoon coconut oil
- 1 medium onion, finely chopped
- 3 garlic cloves, minced
- 1 tablespoon fresh ginger, minced
- 2 tablespoons red curry paste
- 1 can (13.5 oz) coconut milk
- 4 cups vegetable or chicken broth
- 1 tablespoon soy sauce
- 1 tablespoon fish sauce (optional)
- 1 medium carrot, sliced thinly
- 1 bell pepper, thinly sliced
- 1 cup mushrooms, sliced
- 1 cup baby spinach or bok choy
- 1 lime, juiced
- Fresh cilantro, chopped (for garnish)
- Cooked rice or noodles (optional, for serving)

Materials:

- Large pot
- Knife
- Cutting board
- Spoon or ladle

Procedure:

1. Sauté Aromatics: In a large pot, heat the coconut oil over medium heat. Add the chopped onion and sauté until translucent, about 5 minutes. Add the minced garlic and ginger, and cook for another 1-2 minutes until fragrant.

2. Add Curry Paste: Stir in the red curry paste and cook for 1-2 minutes, allowing the flavors to meld and the paste to deepen in color.

3. Incorporate Liquids: Pour in the coconut milk and vegetable or chicken broth, stirring to combine. Bring the mixture to a gentle simmer.

4. Add Vegetables: Add the sliced carrot, bell pepper, and mushrooms to the pot. Simmer for 10-15 minutes, or until the vegetables are tender.

5. Season: Stir in the soy sauce and fish sauce (if using). Adjust seasoning with additional soy sauce or salt to taste.

6. Finish Soup: Add the baby spinach or bok choy and cook for another 1-2 minutes until wilted. Stir in the lime juice just before serving.

7. Serve: Ladle the soup into bowls. Garnish with fresh cilantro and serve with cooked rice or noodles if desired.

Nutritional Value (Per Serving, assuming 4 servings):

- Calories: 220
- Protein: 4g
- Carbohydrates: 18g
- Fat: 15g
- Fiber: 3g

Recipe 20: Caprese Stuffed Chicken Breast

Serves: 4

Preparation time: 15 minutes

Cooking time: 25 minutes

Category: Main Course

Imagine tender, juicy chicken breasts filled with a burst of Italian flavors. This Caprese Stuffed Chicken Breast takes a classic Caprese salad and turns it into a hearty, mouthwatering meal. Picture slicing into the succulent chicken and discovering a gooey, cheesy center with vibrant tomatoes and fresh basil. It's like a slice of Italy on your plate, perfect for a weeknight dinner or a special occasion. With a few simple ingredients, you can elevate a basic chicken breast into a gourmet dish that's sure to impress.

Ingredients:

- 4 boneless, skinless chicken breasts
- 1 cup cherry tomatoes, halved
- 1 cup fresh mozzarella, cubed
- 1/2 cup fresh basil leaves, chopped
- 2 tablespoons balsamic glaze
- 2 tablespoons olive oil
- 1 teaspoon dried oregano
- 1 teaspoon garlic powder
- Salt and black pepper to taste
- Toothpicks or kitchen twine

Materials:

- Baking dish
- Knife
- Cutting board
- Toothpicks or kitchen twine
- Small bowl
- Brush or spoon for balsamic glaze

Procedure:

1. **Preheat Oven:** Preheat your oven to 375°F (190°C). Lightly grease a baking dish.
2. **Prepare Chicken:** Using a sharp knife, carefully cut a pocket into each chicken breast. Be careful not to cut all the way through.

3. **Stuff the Chicken:** In a small bowl, mix the cherry tomatoes, mozzarella, and chopped basil. Stuff each chicken breast with the tomato and cheese mixture. Secure the openings with toothpicks or kitchen twine.

4. **Season:** Drizzle olive oil over the stuffed chicken breasts. Season with dried oregano, garlic powder, salt, and black pepper.

5. **Bake:** Place the stuffed chicken breasts in the prepared baking dish. Bake for 25-30 minutes, or until the chicken is cooked through and reaches an internal temperature of 165°F (74°C). The cheese should be melted and bubbly.

6. **Glaze and Serve:** Drizzle balsamic glaze over the cooked chicken breasts before serving. Remove toothpicks or twine. Serve hot, garnished with additional fresh basil if desired.

Nutritional Value (Per Serving, assuming 4 servings):

- Calories: 330
- Protein: 30g
- Carbohydrates: 6g
- Fat: 20g
- Fiber: 1g

Recipe 21: Korean Bibimbap

Serves: 4

Preparation time: 20 minutes

Cooking time: 30 minutes

Category: Main Course

Bibimbap, a traditional Korean dish, is a vibrant mix of flavors and textures, all harmoniously combined in one bowl. This recipe is your passport to a bustling Korean market, where fresh ingredients and bold spices come together in a dance of culinary delight. Imagine a colorful bowl of Bibimbap, with its mix of savory meats, crisp vegetables, and a perfectly fried egg on top. Each bite is a symphony of taste, bringing a touch of Korean street food magic to your dining table.

Ingredients:

- 1 cup cooked white or brown rice
- 1 tablespoon vegetable oil
- 1/2 pound ground beef or sliced beef (sirloin or ribeye)
- 1 tablespoon soy sauce
- 1 tablespoon sesame oil
- 2 tablespoons gochujang (Korean red chili paste)
- 1 tablespoon sugar
- 1 clove garlic, minced
- 1 medium carrot, julienned
- 1 cup spinach
- 1 cup bean sprouts
- 1 small zucchini, julienned
- 1 tablespoon sesame seeds
- 1-2 eggs (one per serving)
- Sliced green onions and fresh cilantro (for garnish)

Materials:

- Large skillet
- Small pot
- Knife
- Cutting board
- Bowl

Procedure:

1. **Prepare Beef:** In a large skillet over medium heat, add the vegetable oil. Add the ground beef and cook until browned. Stir in the soy sauce, sesame oil, gochujang, sugar, and minced garlic. Cook for an additional 2-3 minutes until well combined and flavorful. Remove from heat and set aside.

2. **Cook Vegetables:**
   - **Carrot and Zucchini:** In the same skillet, add a bit more oil if needed and sauté the julienned carrot and zucchini separately until tender, about 3-4 minutes each. Remove from heat and set aside.
   - **Spinach:** Blanch the spinach in boiling water for about 1 minute, then drain and squeeze out excess moisture. Toss with a little sesame oil and a pinch of salt.
   - **Bean Sprouts:** Briefly blanch the bean sprouts in boiling water for 1-2 minutes, then drain and set aside.

3. **Fry Eggs:** In a separate small skillet, heat a small amount of oil over medium heat. Fry the eggs sunny-side up until the whites are set but the yolk remains runny.

4. **Assemble Bibimbap:** Place a serving of rice in each bowl. Arrange a portion of each cooked vegetable and the beef around the rice, creating a colorful and appetizing presentation. Top each bowl with a fried egg.

5. **Garnish and Serve:** Sprinkle sesame seeds, sliced green onions, and fresh cilantro over the top. Serve with extra gochujang and sesame oil on the side for additional flavor.

Nutritional Value (Per Serving, assuming 4 servings):

- Calories: 450
- Protein: 22g
- Carbohydrates: 55g
- Fat: 16g
- Fiber: 5g

Recipe 22: Greek Lemon Chicken Souvlaki

Serves: 4

Preparation time: 15 minutes

Marinating time: 1-2 hours

Cooking time: 15 minutes

Category: Main Course

Picture yourself by the crystal-clear waters of the Mediterranean, the scent of lemon and oregano filling the air as tender pieces of chicken roast over an open flame. Greek Lemon Chicken Souvla is a celebration of rustic, simple flavors that come together to create a dish worthy of a summer feast. Perfectly charred on the outside and juicy on the inside, this dish will transport you to the sun-drenched islands of Greece with each bite.

Ingredients:

- 4 chicken thighs (bone-in, skin-on)
- 1/4 cup olive oil
- 2 lemons (juice and zest)
- 3 cloves garlic, minced
- 1 tablespoon dried oregano
- 1 tablespoon fresh thyme (or dried)
- Salt and pepper to taste
- 1/2 teaspoon paprika
- Wooden or metal skewers (if grilling)

Materials:

- Large mixing bowl
- Skewers
- Grill or oven

Procedure:

1. **Marinate the Chicken:** In a large bowl, whisk together olive oil, lemon juice, lemon zest, minced garlic, oregano, thyme, salt, pepper,

and paprika. Add the chicken thighs and coat well in the marinade. Cover and let the chicken marinate for at least 1 hour, or up to overnight for the best flavor.

2. **Prepare the Grill or Oven:** If grilling, preheat the grill to medium-high heat. If roasting, preheat the oven to 400°F (200°C).

3. **Cook the Chicken:** Thread the marinated chicken onto skewers if using a grill. Grill or roast for 20-25 minutes, turning occasionally, until the chicken is golden and fully cooked through, with an internal temperature of 165°F (75°C).

4. **Serve:** Serve the chicken with a side of pita, tzatziki sauce, and a Greek salad, or simply garnish with lemon wedges and fresh herbs.

Nutritional Value (Per Serving):

- Calories: 320
- Protein: 24g
- Carbohydrates: 5g
- Fat: 23g

Recipe 23: Vietnamese Pho

Serves: 4

Preparation time: 20 minutes

Cooking time: 3 hours

Category: Main Course (Soup)

Pho is more than just a dish—it's a soul-soothing experience. Imagine a bustling street in Hanoi, where the aroma of simmering broth mingles with the scent of fresh herbs. This classic Vietnamese soup, with its rich broth and delicate noodles, is the epitome of comfort. Each spoonful delivers warmth, flavor, and the satisfaction that only a slow-cooked, aromatic soup can provide.

Ingredients:

- 1 pound beef bones (marrow or knuckle bones)
- 1/2 pound beef brisket
- 1 onion, halved
- 2-inch piece of ginger, sliced
- 2 star anise
- 4 cloves
- 1 cinnamon stick
- 4 cloves garlic
- 1 tablespoon fish sauce
- 8 cups water
- 1 tablespoon sugar
- 8 ounces rice noodles (pho noodles)
- 1/2 pound beef sirloin, thinly sliced
- Fresh herbs (cilantro, basil, mint)
- Bean sprouts
- 1 lime, cut into wedges
- Fresh chili slices (optional)
- Hoisin sauce and Sriracha (for serving)

Materials:

- Large pot
- Mesh strainer
- Ladle

Procedure:

1. **Roast Aromatics:** Heat a large pot over medium-high heat. Add the onion and ginger, roasting until charred. Add star anise, cloves, cinnamon stick, and garlic. Toast the spices for 1-2 minutes, until fragrant.

2. **Prepare Broth:** Add the beef bones, brisket, fish sauce, sugar, and water to the pot. Bring to a boil, then reduce to a simmer. Let the broth simmer for at least 4-5 hours (or longer for a richer flavor), skimming any impurities that rise to the top.

3. **Cook Noodles:** Cook the pho noodles according to package instructions. Drain and set aside.

4. **Assemble the Pho:** Place a handful of noodles in each bowl, followed by thin slices of raw beef sirloin. Ladle the hot broth over the beef, cooking it instantly in the bowl. Add cooked brisket slices as well.

5. **Garnish and Serve:** Top each bowl with fresh herbs, bean sprouts, lime wedges, and chili slices. Serve with hoisin sauce and Sriracha on the side.

Nutritional Value (Per Serving):

- Calories: 400
- Protein: 30g
- Carbohydrates: 45g
- Fat: 10g

Recipe 24: Mexican Street Corn (Elote)

Serves: 4

Preparation time: 10 minutes

Cooking time: 15 minutes

Category: Appetizer/Side Dish

Imagine walking through the vibrant streets of Mexico City, where food vendors line the sidewalks, serving up smoky, grilled elote slathered in rich, tangy toppings. Mexican street corn is a true celebration of flavor—smoky, creamy, tangy, and slightly spicy, all wrapped around sweet, charred corn on the cob. It's a handheld treat that brings the taste of Mexico right to your kitchen.

Ingredients:

- 4 ears of corn, husked
- 1/4 cup mayonnaise
- 1/4 cup sour cream
- 1/2 cup cotija cheese, crumbled
- 1 teaspoon chili powder
- 1 lime, cut into wedges
- Fresh cilantro, chopped (optional)
- Salt to taste

Materials:

- Grill or stovetop grill pan
- Tongs
- Small bowl
- Brush for spreading toppings

Procedure:

1. **Grill the Corn:** Preheat the grill to medium-high heat. Place the corn directly on the grill and cook, turning occasionally, until the kernels are charred in spots and fully cooked—about 8-10 minutes.
2. **Prepare the Toppings:** In a small bowl, mix together the mayonnaise, sour cream, and a pinch of salt. Set aside.
3. **Coat the Corn:** Using a brush or spoon, generously spread the mayonnaise mixture over each ear of corn while it's still warm.
4. **Add the Finishing Touches:** Sprinkle crumbled cotija cheese over the corn, followed by a dusting of chili powder. Garnish with fresh

cilantro if desired, and serve with lime wedges for an extra burst of tang.

5. **Enjoy:** Dig in with your hands and squeeze a little lime over the top for that authentic Mexican street food experience.

Nutritional Value (Per Serving):

- Calories: 280
- Protein: 7g
- Carbohydrates: 31g
- Fat: 16g
- Fiber: 4g

Recipe 25: Japanese Matcha Green Tea Latte

Serves: 2

Preparation time: 5 minutes

Cooking time: 5 minutes

Category: Beverage

Transport yourself to a serene Japanese tea house, where the ceremonial art of preparing matcha brings a moment of tranquility and mindfulness. This Matcha Green Tea Latte combines the earthy, vibrant flavor of matcha with creamy milk for a perfectly balanced drink that's both energizing and soothing. Whether you're looking to start your day with focus or unwind in the afternoon, this latte is the answer.

Ingredients:

- 1 teaspoon matcha green tea powder
- 1/4 cup hot water (not boiling)
- 3/4 cup milk (dairy or plant-based)
- 1 teaspoon honey or maple syrup (optional)
- Ice cubes (for iced version)

Materials:

- Matcha whisk or regular whisk
- Small bowl
- Milk frother (optional)

Procedure:

1. **Prepare the Matcha:** In a small bowl, sift the matcha powder to remove any lumps. Add the hot water (about 175°F) and whisk

vigorously in a zig-zag motion until the matcha is fully dissolved and frothy.

2. **Heat the Milk:** Warm the milk in a small saucepan over medium heat, or use a milk frother to heat and froth it. If making an iced version, skip this step and pour cold milk over ice instead.

3. **Sweeten (Optional):** If desired, stir honey or maple syrup into the matcha mixture to sweeten the latte.

4. **Combine:** Pour the matcha mixture into a cup and slowly add the warm frothed milk. For an iced version, pour the matcha over ice, followed by cold milk.

5. **Serve:** Give it a gentle stir and enjoy your creamy, vibrant green tea latte, perfect for sipping mindfully.

Nutritional Value (Per Serving):

- Calories: 100
- Protein: 4g
- Carbohydrates: 12g
- Fat: 4g
- Fiber: 1g

Recipe 26: Moroccan Chicken Tagine

Serves: 4

Preparation time: 20 minutes

Cooking time: 1 hour

Category: Entrée

Picture the bustling souks of Marrakech, where the scent of exotic spices fills the air, and the warmth of tagines cooking slowly over coals draws people in. Moroccan Chicken Tagine is more than just a dish—it's a journey into the heart of North African cuisine. With tender chicken, dried fruits, and fragrant spices, this dish is a balance of sweet and savory that's sure to transport you with every bite.

Ingredients:

- 4 chicken thighs (bone-in, skin-on)
- 1 onion, diced
- 2 cloves garlic, minced
- 1 teaspoon ground cumin
- 1 teaspoon ground coriander
- 1 teaspoon ground cinnamon
- 1/2 teaspoon ground ginger
- 1/2 teaspoon turmeric
- 1 cup chicken broth
- 1/2 cup dried apricots, halved
- 1/4 cup raisins
- 1 can chickpeas, drained and rinsed
- 1/4 cup fresh cilantro, chopped
- Olive oil
- Salt and pepper to taste

Materials:

- Tagine pot or heavy-bottomed pot with a lid
- Wooden spoon
- Measuring cups and spoons

Procedure:

1. **Sear the Chicken:** Heat a drizzle of olive oil in the tagine or pot over medium heat. Season the chicken thighs with salt and pepper,

then sear them skin-side down until golden and crispy, about 5 minutes. Flip and cook for another 3 minutes, then set aside.

2. **Sauté the Aromatics:** In the same pot, add the onions and garlic, cooking until soft and fragrant. Stir in the cumin, coriander, cinnamon, ginger, and turmeric, cooking for another minute to bloom the spices.

3. **Simmer:** Add the chicken broth, apricots, raisins, and chickpeas to the pot. Return the chicken to the pot, nestling it into the liquid. Bring to a simmer, then cover and cook on low heat for 35-40 minutes, until the chicken is tender and cooked through.

4. **Finish:** Remove the lid and allow the sauce to thicken slightly, if necessary. Stir in fresh cilantro, adjust seasoning with salt and pepper, and serve over couscous or rice.

5. **Serve:** Garnish with extra cilantro and serve warm, enjoying the rich, aromatic flavors of Morocco.

Nutritional Value (Per Serving):

- Calories: 420
- Protein: 25g
- Carbohydrates: 40g
- Fat: 18g
- Fiber: 7g

Recipe 27: Thai Mango Sticky Rice

Serves: 4

Preparation time: 10 minutes

Cooking time: 20 minutes

Category: Dessert

Close your eyes and imagine strolling through a Thai night market, where vendors offer sweet treats and tropical fruits in every corner. Thai Mango Sticky Rice is a beloved street food dessert, featuring the creamy richness of coconut-infused sticky rice paired with the juicy sweetness of ripe mango. It's a symphony of flavors and textures—a must-try for anyone who loves a perfect balance of sweetness and creaminess.

Ingredients:

- 1 cup glutinous (sticky) rice
- 1 1/4 cups coconut milk
- 1/4 cup sugar
- 1/4 teaspoon salt
- 2 ripe mangoes, peeled and sliced
- 1 tablespoon sesame seeds (optional)

Materials:

- Rice steamer or pot with a steamer basket
- Small saucepan
- Mixing bowl
- Serving plates

Procedure:

1. **Cook the Sticky Rice:** Rinse the sticky rice under cold water until the water runs clear. Soak the rice for 30 minutes, then steam it in a rice steamer for about 20-25 minutes until fully cooked and tender.

2. **Prepare the Coconut Sauce:** While the rice steams, heat the coconut milk, sugar, and salt in a small saucepan over low heat. Stir until the sugar dissolves, then remove from heat. Set aside 1/4 cup of the sauce for drizzling.

3. **Combine:** Once the rice is done, transfer it to a mixing bowl and slowly pour the remaining coconut sauce over the rice. Stir to combine, letting the rice absorb the sauce for 10 minutes.

4. **Assemble:** To serve, shape the sticky rice into mounds on plates, then place slices of ripe mango alongside. Drizzle the reserved coconut sauce over the rice and sprinkle with sesame seeds, if using.

5. **Enjoy:** Serve immediately and savor the tropical sweetness of this traditional Thai dessert.

Nutritional Value (Per Serving):

- Calories: 340
- Protein: 4g
- Carbohydrates: 66g
- Fat: 8g
- Fiber: 3g

Recipe 28: Italian Caprese Salad

Serves: 4

Preparation time: 10 minutes

Category: Appetizer

Imagine yourself in the heart of Italy, where simplicity and flavor are celebrated in every dish. The Caprese Salad, a tribute to the island of Capri, embodies the essence of Italian cuisine with its vibrant colors, fresh ingredients, and perfect balance. This dish showcases the best of summer with ripe tomatoes, creamy mozzarella, and fragrant basil drizzled with olive oil—each bite is like a taste of the Mediterranean.

Ingredients:

- 3 ripe tomatoes, sliced
- 8 oz fresh mozzarella, sliced
- 1/4 cup fresh basil leaves
- 2 tbsp extra virgin olive oil
- 1 tbsp balsamic glaze
- Salt and pepper to taste

Materials:

- Cutting board
- Sharp knife
- Serving plate

Procedure:

1. **Prepare the Ingredients:** Slice the tomatoes and mozzarella into even rounds. Pick fresh basil leaves from the stems.

2. **Assemble the Salad:** On a serving plate, alternate slices of tomato and mozzarella, layering them in a circle or row. Tuck basil leaves between each slice.

3. **Drizzle:** Drizzle olive oil and balsamic glaze over the salad, making sure to coat each layer for added flavor.

4. **Season:** Sprinkle with a generous pinch of salt and freshly ground black pepper to taste.

5. **Serve:** Serve immediately and enjoy this fresh, authentic Italian appetizer that captures the flavors of summer.

Nutritional Value (Per Serving):

- Calories: 250
- Protein: 12g
- Carbohydrates: 7g
- Fat: 20g
- Fiber: 2g

Recipe 29: Indian Butter Chicken (Murgh Makhani)

Serves: 4

Preparation time: 15 minutes

Cooking time: 30 minutes

Category: Entrée

From the kitchens of Delhi to tables worldwide, Butter Chicken has become a beloved symbol of Indian cuisine. Rich, creamy, and brimming with fragrant spices, this dish is a fusion of flavors that brings comfort and warmth. The tender chicken is marinated in a spiced yogurt blend and cooked in a luscious tomato-cream sauce that makes every bite feel indulgent yet familiar.

Ingredients:

- 1 lb boneless chicken thighs, cut into bite-sized pieces
- 1 cup plain yogurt
- 2 tbsp lemon juice
- 2 tsp garam masala
- 1 tsp ground cumin
- 1 tsp ground coriander
- 1 tsp ground turmeric
- 1/2 tsp chili powder
- 4 tbsp butter
- 1 onion, finely chopped
- 2 garlic cloves, minced
- 1-inch piece ginger, minced
- 1 cup tomato purée
- 1/2 cup heavy cream
- Salt to taste
- Fresh cilantro for garnish

Materials:

- Large mixing bowl
- Skillet or large pan
- Wooden spoon

Procedure:

1. **Marinate the Chicken:** In a large bowl, combine yogurt, lemon juice, garam masala, cumin, coriander, turmeric, and chili powder.

Add the chicken pieces and marinate for at least 30 minutes (overnight for best results).

2. **Cook the Chicken:** Heat 2 tbsp of butter in a skillet over medium heat. Add the marinated chicken and cook until browned and cooked through, about 6-8 minutes. Remove and set aside.

3. **Sauté the Aromatics:** In the same skillet, melt the remaining butter and add chopped onion, garlic, and ginger. Sauté until soft and fragrant.

4. **Make the Sauce:** Stir in the tomato purée and cook for about 10 minutes until it thickens. Reduce the heat and slowly pour in the cream, stirring until the sauce is smooth and creamy.

5. **Finish the Dish:** Return the chicken to the pan, stirring to coat in the sauce. Simmer for 10 minutes, allowing the flavors to meld. Adjust seasoning with salt.

6. **Serve:** Garnish with fresh cilantro and serve over basmati rice or with warm naan bread.

Nutritional Value (Per Serving):

- Calories: 480
- Protein: 25g
- Carbohydrates: 10g
- Fat: 36g
- Fiber: 2g

Recipe 30: Mexican Churros

Serves: 4

Preparation time: 15 minutes

Cooking time: 20 minutes

Category: Dessert

A visit to any Mexican festival wouldn't be complete without the sweet, crispy joy of churros. Fried to golden perfection and dusted in cinnamon sugar, these traditional treats are a crunchy, sugary delight. Paired with a rich chocolate dipping sauce, churros are the ultimate indulgence—a treat that makes you feel like a kid again with every bite.

Ingredients:

- 1 cup water
- 2 tbsp sugar
- 2 tbsp butter
- 1 cup all-purpose flour
- 1/4 tsp salt
- 1 egg
- 1/2 tsp vanilla extract
- Vegetable oil for frying
- 1/2 cup sugar (for coating)
- 1 tsp ground cinnamon

Materials:

- Medium saucepan
- Piping bag with star tip
- Deep fryer or large pot
- Paper towels

Procedure:

1. **Prepare the Dough:** In a medium saucepan, bring water, sugar, butter, and salt to a boil. Remove from heat and stir in flour until a smooth dough forms. Let it cool slightly, then beat in the egg and vanilla extract until fully incorporated.

2. **Heat the Oil:** In a deep fryer or large pot, heat oil to 350°F (175°C). The oil should be deep enough for frying the churros.

3. **Pipe the Churros:** Transfer the dough into a piping bag fitted with a star tip. Pipe 4-5 inch lengths of dough into the hot oil, using scissors to cut them off. Fry until golden brown, about 3-4 minutes per side.

4. **Coat in Cinnamon Sugar:** Drain the churros on paper towels, then roll them in the cinnamon sugar mixture while still warm.

5. **Serve:** Serve with chocolate sauce or dulce de leche for dipping, and enjoy this crispy, sweet Mexican classic.

Nutritional Value (Per Serving):

- Calories: 250
- Protein: 3g
- Carbohydrates: 25g
- Fat: 15g
- Fiber: 1g

Recipe 31: Korean Bibimbap

Serves: 4

Preparation time: 30 minutes

Cooking time: 30 minutes

Category: Entrée

Bibimbap is more than just a dish—it's a vibrant celebration of color, texture, and flavor that embodies the harmony of Korean cuisine. Imagine sitting in a bustling Seoul street market, the sizzling sound of fresh ingredients hitting a hot stone bowl. Bibimbap, meaning "mixed rice," is an artistic blend of vegetables, protein, and rice, all brought together with the bold kick of gochujang (Korean chili paste). This dish is as visually stunning as it is delicious, offering a balance of savory, spicy, and umami in every bite.

Ingredients:

- 2 cups cooked white rice
- 1/2 lb beef (or tofu), thinly sliced
- 1 tbsp soy sauce
- 1 tsp sesame oil
- 1 garlic clove, minced
- 1 carrot, julienned
- 1 zucchini, julienned
- 1 cup spinach, blanched
- 4 shiitake mushrooms, sliced
- 1 tbsp vegetable oil
- 1 egg (per serving)
- 2 tbsp gochujang (Korean chili paste)
- 1 tbsp sesame seeds
- Kimchi for serving (optional)

Materials:

- Large skillet or wok
- Small saucepan
- Mixing bowls

- Spoon

Procedure:

1. Prepare the Beef: In a bowl, marinate the thinly sliced beef (or tofu) with soy sauce, sesame oil, and minced garlic for 10 minutes.
2. Sauté the Vegetables: Heat vegetable oil in a skillet. Sauté the carrots, zucchini, mushrooms, and spinach separately until tender, seasoning each with a pinch of salt. Set aside.
3. Cook the Beef: In the same skillet, cook the marinated beef or tofu until browned and cooked through. Remove and set aside.
4. Fry the Egg: In a small saucepan, fry the egg sunny side up, ensuring the yolk stays runny.
5. Assemble the Bibimbap: In a large bowl, start with a base of warm cooked rice. Arrange the sautéed vegetables, cooked beef, and fried egg on top in sections, creating a colorful presentation.
6. Garnish: Add a dollop of gochujang in the center, sprinkle with sesame seeds, and serve with a side of kimchi if desired.
7. Mix and Enjoy: Before eating, mix everything together with a spoon, allowing the flavors and textures to combine for the ultimate Korean dining experience.

Nutritional Value (Per Serving):

- Calories: 450
- Protein: 20g
- Carbohydrates: 45g

- Fat: 20g
- Fiber: 6g

Recipe 32: Greek Moussaka

Serves: 6

Preparation time: 1 hour

Cooking time: 1 hour

Category: Entrée

Moussaka is the heart and soul of Greek comfort food, a dish that transports you to a rustic taverna overlooking the Aegean Sea. Layers of rich, spiced meat sauce, tender eggplant, and creamy béchamel create a hearty, flavor-packed casserole that's perfect for family gatherings. Each bite offers a taste of Greece's culinary tradition, bringing together bold Mediterranean spices, fresh vegetables, and a luxurious sauce.

Ingredients:

- 2 large eggplants, sliced
- 1 lb ground lamb or beef
- 1 onion, finely chopped
- 2 cloves garlic, minced
- 1 can (14 oz) crushed tomatoes
- 1 tsp ground cinnamon
- 1 tsp dried oregano
- 1/4 cup red wine
- 1/4 cup grated Parmesan cheese
- 4 tbsp olive oil
- 2 tbsp butter
- 2 tbsp flour
- 2 cups milk
- Salt and pepper to taste

Materials:

- Skillet
- Saucepan
- Baking dish
- Whisk

Procedure:

1. **Prepare the Eggplant:** Lightly salt the eggplant slices and let them sit for 20 minutes to draw out moisture. Pat dry and fry in olive oil until golden brown. Set aside.

2. **Make the Meat Sauce:** In a skillet, sauté onions and garlic until softened. Add the ground meat, browning it well. Stir in crushed tomatoes, cinnamon, oregano, and red wine, letting it simmer until thickened. Season with salt and pepper.

3. **Prepare the Béchamel:** In a saucepan, melt butter and whisk in flour to form a roux. Gradually add milk, whisking constantly until the sauce thickens. Stir in Parmesan cheese and a pinch of nutmeg.

4. **Assemble the Moussaka:** In a baking dish, layer half the eggplant, followed by the meat sauce, then the remaining eggplant. Pour the béchamel sauce over the top, spreading evenly.

5. **Bake:** Bake at 350°F for 45 minutes until golden brown on top. Let it cool slightly before serving.

Nutritional Value (Per Serving):

- Calories: 400
- Protein: 20g
- Carbohydrates: 30g
- Fat: 22g
- Fiber: 8g

Recipe 33: Japanese Tempura

Serves: 4

Preparation time: 20 minutes

Cooking time: 20 minutes

Category: Appetizer

Tempura is a celebration of delicate flavors and textures, where the crispiness of light batter meets the freshness of seafood and vegetables. Imagine sitting in a serene Japanese garden, enjoying perfectly fried tempura as the breeze gently rustles through bamboo. With this recipe, you'll learn the art of frying like a true Japanese chef—light, airy, and golden perfection in every bite.

Ingredients:

- 10 large shrimp, peeled and deveined
- 1 sweet potato, thinly sliced
- 1 zucchini, sliced
- 1 cup all-purpose flour
- 1 egg yolk
- 1 cup ice-cold water
- 1/4 cup cornstarch
- Vegetable oil for frying
- Soy sauce or tempura dipping sauce

Materials:

- Deep frying pan
- Mixing bowl
- Tongs

Procedure:

1. **Prepare the Batter:** In a bowl, lightly whisk the egg yolk with ice-cold water. Gradually add flour and cornstarch, mixing gently until just combined—small lumps are fine.
2. **Heat the Oil:** Heat vegetable oil in a deep pan to 350°F.
3. **Coat and Fry:** Dip the shrimp and vegetables in the batter, letting any excess drip off. Fry in small batches until golden and crisp, about 2-3 minutes. Drain on paper towels.
4. **Serve:** Serve hot with soy sauce or a tempura dipping sauce on the side.

Cooking Tips:

- To achieve a light and crispy tempura, make sure the batter is chilled and the oil is hot.
- For a more traditional Japanese touch, you can serve the tempura with grated daikon radish and soy sauce for dipping.

Nutritional Value (Per Serving):

- Calories: 280
- Protein: 15g
- Carbohydrates: 30g
- Fat: 10g
- Fiber: 4g

Recipe 34: Moroccan Chicken Tagine

Serves: 4

Preparation time: 20 minutes

Cooking time: 1 hour 30 minutes

Category: Entrée

Transport yourself to the bustling markets of Marrakech with this fragrant Moroccan Chicken Tagine. With its slow-cooked blend of tender chicken, aromatic spices, and preserved lemons, this dish embodies the warmth and richness of North African cuisine. Each bite is an adventure through layers of flavor, from the earthiness of cumin to the sweetness of dried apricots.

Ingredients:

- 4 chicken thighs, bone-in
- 1 onion, finely chopped
- 2 garlic cloves, minced
- 1 tsp ground cumin
- 1 tsp ground ginger
- 1 tsp ground turmeric
- 1/2 tsp cinnamon
- 1/4 cup dried apricots
- 1/4 cup green olives
- 1 preserved lemon, chopped
- 2 tbsp olive oil
- 1 cup chicken broth
- Fresh cilantro for garnish

Materials:

- Tagine pot or Dutch oven
- Wooden spoon

Procedure:

1. **Sear the Chicken:** Heat olive oil in a tagine or Dutch oven. Brown the chicken thighs on both sides. Remove and set aside.

2. **Sauté the Onion and Spices:** In the same pot, sauté the onion and garlic until soft. Stir in cumin, ginger, turmeric, and cinnamon, cooking until fragrant.

3. **Simmer:** Add the chicken back to the pot, along with dried apricots, olives, preserved lemon, and chicken broth. Cover and let it simmer over low heat for 45 minutes, until the chicken is tender.

4. **Garnish and Serve:** Garnish with fresh cilantro and serve with couscous or flatbread.

Cooking Tips:

- If you don't have a tagine, you can use a Dutch oven or any heavy-bottomed pot with a tight-fitting lid.
- For added depth of flavor, you can marinate the chicken thighs in the spice mixture for a few hours or overnight before cooking.

Nutritional Value (Per Serving):

- Calories: 350
- Protein: 25g
- Carbohydrates: 20g
- Fat: 18g
- Fiber: 6g

Recipe 35: Thai Green Curry

Serves: 4

Preparation time: 15 minutes

Cooking time: 25 minutes

Category: Entrée

Imagine walking through the streets of Bangkok, where the air is fragrant with the smell of fresh lemongrass, coconut milk, and fiery green chilies. Thai Green Curry is an explosion of bold flavors that tantalize your taste buds—spicy, creamy, and herbaceous. It's the kind of dish that warms your soul with every spoonful, offering a true taste of Thailand's culinary magic.

Ingredients:

- 1 lb chicken breast, sliced
- 2 tbsp green curry paste
- 1 can coconut milk (14 oz)
- 1 cup chicken broth
- 1 tbsp fish sauce
- 1 tbsp brown sugar
- 1 cup bamboo shoots
- 1 red bell pepper, sliced
- 1 cup fresh Thai basil leaves
- 2 kaffir lime leaves (optional)
- 1 tbsp vegetable oil
- Cooked jasmine rice for serving

Materials:

- Wok or large skillet
- Wooden spoon

Procedure:

1. **Prepare the Curry Base:** Heat the oil in a wok over medium heat. Add the green curry paste and fry for 1-2 minutes until fragrant.
2. **Cook the Chicken:** Add the sliced chicken and stir-fry until it starts to brown.
3. **Add Liquids and Vegetables:** Pour in the coconut milk and chicken broth. Stir in fish sauce, brown sugar, bamboo shoots, and

red bell pepper. Add kaffir lime leaves if using. Let it simmer for 10 minutes.

4. **Finish with Herbs:** Stir in the fresh Thai basil just before serving. Ladle the curry over jasmine rice.

Cooking Tip: If you want a spicier curry, add fresh Thai chilies while frying the curry paste. For a creamier texture, reduce the curry for a few extra minutes.

Nutritional Value (Per Serving):

- Calories: 450
- Protein: 28g
- Carbohydrates: 20g
- Fat: 30g
- Fiber: 4g

Recipe 36: Indian Butter Chicken (Murgh Makhani)

Serves: 4
Preparation time: 20 minutes
Cooking time: 40 minutes
Category: Entrée

Butter Chicken is the crown jewel of Indian cuisine, a dish beloved for its rich, velvety tomato sauce and succulent pieces of marinated chicken. This recipe takes you straight to the heart of India, where the aromas of cumin, coriander, and fenugreek waft through bustling markets. The comforting flavors of Butter Chicken remind you of the warmth of home and the joy of sharing a delicious meal with loved ones.

Ingredients:

- 1 lb chicken breast, cubed
- 1 cup plain yogurt
- 1 tbsp garam masala
- 1 tbsp turmeric
- 1 tsp cayenne pepper
- 1 tbsp ground cumin
- 4 tbsp butter
- 1 onion, finely chopped
- 3 garlic cloves, minced
- 1 can tomato puree (14 oz)
- 1/2 cup heavy cream
- 1 tbsp sugar
- Salt to taste
- Fresh cilantro for garnish

Materials:

- Large skillet
- Mixing bowl
- Blender (optional)

Procedure:

1. **Marinate the Chicken:** Mix yogurt, garam masala, turmeric, cayenne, and cumin in a bowl. Add chicken, coating it well. Marinate for at least 30 minutes.

2. **Cook the Chicken:** Melt butter in a large skillet over medium heat. Add the marinated chicken and cook until browned. Set aside.

3. **Prepare the Sauce:** In the same skillet, sauté onions and garlic until softened. Add tomato puree, sugar, and salt, cooking for 10 minutes. For a smoother sauce, blend the mixture.

4. **Finish the Dish:** Return the chicken to the skillet, stirring in the heavy cream. Simmer for 10 minutes. Garnish with cilantro.

Cooking Tip: For an extra smoky flavor, char the chicken on a grill or under the broiler before adding it to the sauce.

Nutritional Value (Per Serving):

- Calories: 500
- Protein: 32g
- Carbohydrates: 15g
- Fat: 35g
- Fiber: 3g

Recipe 37: Mexican Tacos al Pastor

Serves: 4

Preparation time: 20 minutes

Marinating time: 2-4 hours

Cooking time: 15 minutes

Category: Entrée

Picture yourself at a lively street food market in Mexico City, where a giant spit of marinated pork rotates slowly, caramelizing under the heat. Tacos al Pastor are a celebration of bold, smoky flavors, with pineapple adding a sweet contrast to the spicy, marinated meat. Each taco is a small, flavorful bite of Mexico, a dish that brings together tradition, community, and the love of good food.

Ingredients:

- 1 lb pork shoulder, thinly sliced
- 1/2 cup pineapple juice
- 2 tbsp achiote paste
- 1 tbsp cumin
- 1 tsp smoked paprika
- 1 tsp chili powder
- 1 tbsp vinegar
- 1/4 cup fresh cilantro, chopped
- 1 pineapple, sliced
- Corn tortillas
- Lime wedges for serving

Materials:

- Grill or stovetop skillet
- Mixing bowl

Procedure:

1. Marinate the Pork: In a bowl, combine pineapple juice, achiote paste, cumin, paprika, chili powder, and vinegar. Add the pork, coating thoroughly. Marinate for at least 1 hour.

2. Cook the Pork: Grill the marinated pork slices on high heat until slightly charred. Grill the pineapple slices alongside until caramelized.

3. Assemble the Tacos: Warm the tortillas and fill with pork, grilled pineapple, and cilantro. Serve with lime wedges.

4. Cooking Tip: For a more authentic al pastor experience, cook the pork on a vertical rotisserie if available, or simply grill on skewers.

Cooking Tips:

- For an authentic touch, you can also add a small slice of pineapple to the tacos along with the pork.

- If you don't have access to a grill or skillet, you can also cook the marinated pork in the oven at 400°F (200°C) for about 15 minutes or until cooked through.

Nutritional Value (Per Serving):

- Calories: 350
- Protein: 20g
- Carbohydrates: 28g
- Fat: 15g
- Fiber: 4g

Recipe 38: Vietnamese Pho

Serves: 4

Preparation time: 20 minutes

Cooking time: 3 hours

Category: Entrée

Pho is Vietnam in a bowl. Imagine sitting in a small roadside café in Hanoi, the steam from a fragrant broth rising in front of you. With its delicate blend of star anise, cinnamon, and clove, Pho is more than just a noodle soup—it's a meditative experience, a slow-brewed dish that captures the essence of Vietnamese culture in each sip. Every spoonful feels like a warm embrace from the streets of Vietnam.

Ingredients:

- 1 lb beef bones (or chicken bones)
- 1 onion, halved
- 4-inch piece of ginger, sliced
- 2 cinnamon sticks
- 3 star anise pods
- 4 cloves
- 1 tbsp fish sauce
- 1 tbsp sugar
- 8 oz rice noodles
- 8 oz beef sirloin, thinly sliced
- Fresh basil, cilantro, and bean sprouts for garnish
- Lime wedges for serving

Materials:

- Stockpot
- Strainer

Procedure:

1. **Prepare the Broth:** In a stockpot, char the onion and ginger over high heat until blackened. Add bones, cinnamon, star anise, cloves, fish sauce, sugar, and water to cover. Simmer for 4 hours.

2. **Cook the Noodles:** Cook the rice noodles according to package instructions. Drain and set aside.

3. **Assemble the Pho:** In a bowl, add the cooked noodles and raw beef slices. Ladle the hot broth over to cook the beef. Garnish with fresh herbs and serve with lime wedges.

Cooking Tip: Blanch the bones before simmering to remove impurities and ensure a clear broth.

Nutritional Value (Per Serving):

- Calories: 400
- Protein: 25g
- Carbohydrates: 40g
- Fat: 12g
- Fiber: 2g

Recipe 39: Italian Tiramisu

Serves: 6-8

Preparation time: 30 minutes

Chilling time: 4 hours or overnight

Category: Dessert

Tiramisu is Italy's answer to the perfect dessert, a delicate dance of espresso-soaked ladyfingers, rich mascarpone cream, and a dusting of cocoa. It transports you to a cozy Italian café, where the hum of conversation mixes with the aroma of freshly brewed coffee. With each bite, you'll feel as though you've taken a mini escape to the rolling hills of Tuscany.

Ingredients:

- 1 cup strong brewed espresso
- 2 tbsp rum (optional)
- 4 egg yolks
- 1/2 cup sugar
- 8 oz mascarpone cheese
- 1 cup heavy cream, whipped
- 24 ladyfingers
- Cocoa powder for dusting

Materials:

- Mixing bowls
- Whisk

Procedure:

1. **Prepare the Coffee Mixture:** Mix the espresso and rum in a shallow bowl. Set aside.
2. **Make the Mascarpone Filling:** In a bowl, whisk egg yolks and sugar over a double boiler until thick. Remove from heat and fold in mascarpone cheese, then gently fold in the whipped cream.
3. **Assemble the Tiramisu:** Dip ladyfingers into the coffee mixture and layer them in a dish. Spread the mascarpone mixture over the top. Repeat with another layer. Dust with cocoa powder.

4. **Chill:** Refrigerate for at least 4 hours before serving.

Cooking Tips:

- For a richer flavor, prepare the tiramisu a day ahead to let the flavors fully meld.
- For a non-alcoholic version, you can omit the coffee liqueur or substitute it with a coffee-flavored syrup.
- Tiramisu is best made a day in advance to allow the flavors to develop and the ladyfingers to soften.

Nutritional Value (Per Serving):

- Calories: 450
- Protein: 8g
- Carbohydrates: 40g
- Fat: 30g
- Fiber: 2g

Recipe 40: Korean Bibimbap

Serves: 4

Preparation time: 30 minutes

Cooking time: 30 minutes

Category: Entrée

Bibimbap is the ultimate Korean comfort food, a vibrant bowl bursting with fresh vegetables, savory beef, and a runny egg, all mixed together with gochujang. It's the perfect balance of flavors and textures—a little bit of heat, a little bit of sweetness, and a lot of crunch. This dish captures the essence of Korean home cooking, where health, flavor, and satisfaction come together in one harmonious bowl.

Ingredients:

- 2 cups cooked white rice
- 1/2 lb beef sirloin, thinly sliced
- 1 tbsp soy sauce
- 1 tbsp sesame oil
- 1 garlic clove, minced
- 1 carrot, julienned
- 1 zucchini, julienned
- 1 cup spinach, blanched
- 1/2 cup bean sprouts, blanched
- 1 egg (per serving)
- 1 tbsp gochujang (Korean chili paste)
- 1 tsp sesame seeds for garnish
- Fresh cucumber and radish for garnish

Materials:

- Large skillet or wok
- Mixing bowls

Procedure:

1. **Marinate the Beef:** In a bowl, combine soy sauce, sesame oil, and minced garlic. Add the beef slices and let them marinate for 30 minutes.

2. **Cook the Vegetables**: Sauté the carrots, zucchini, spinach, and bean sprouts separately in a little sesame oil, seasoning lightly with salt. Set each aside.

3. **Cook the Beef**: In the same skillet, cook the marinated beef until browned.

4. **Fry the Egg**: In a separate small pan, fry each egg sunny-side up.

5. **Assemble the Bibimbap**: In a bowl, place a base of steamed rice. Arrange the vegetables, beef, and egg on top in sections. Add a spoonful of gochujang in the center and sprinkle with sesame seeds.

6. **Serve**: Mix everything together right before eating to combine the flavors.

Cooking Tips:

- For an extra crispy texture, use a stone pot (dolsot) to cook the rice, creating a golden, crunchy layer at the bottom.
- For extra flavor, you can drizzle a little sesame oil over the assembled bibimbap before serving.
- Feel free to customize the mixed vegetables based on your preferences and seasonal availability.

Nutritional Value (Per Serving):

- Calories: 500
- Protein: 25g
- Carbohydrates: 55g
- Fat: 18g
- Fiber: 6g

Recipe 41: Thai Green Curry

Serves: 4

Preparation time: 15 minutes

Cooking time: 20 minutes

Category: Entrée

Thai Green Curry is a symphony of vibrant colors and bold flavors, capturing the essence of Thailand's rich culinary heritage. Imagine the bustling streets of Bangkok, where the air is filled with the aromatic scents of lemongrass, kaffir lime, and fresh chilies. This curry combines tender pieces of chicken with an array of vegetables in a creamy coconut milk base, creating a harmonious balance of spicy, sweet, and savory notes that dance on your palate.

Ingredients:

- 1 lb chicken breast, thinly sliced
- 2 tbsp green curry paste
- 1 can (14 oz) coconut milk
- 1 cup chicken broth

- 1 tbsp fish sauce
- 1 tbsp brown sugar
- 1 cup bamboo shoots
- 1 red bell pepper, sliced
- 1 cup Thai basil leaves
- 2 kaffir lime leaves (optional)
- 1 tbsp vegetable oil
- Cooked jasmine rice for serving

Materials:

- Wok or large skillet
- Wooden spoon
- Measuring cups and spoons

Procedure:

1. **Prepare the Curry Base**: Heat the vegetable oil in a wok over medium heat. Add the green curry paste and sauté for 1-2 minutes until fragrant.

2. **Cook the Chicken**: Add the sliced chicken to the wok and stir-fry until it starts to brown.

3. **Add Liquids and Vegetables**: Pour in the coconut milk and chicken broth. Stir in the fish sauce, brown sugar, bamboo shoots, and red bell pepper. Add the kaffir lime leaves if using. Bring to a simmer and let it cook for 10 minutes.

4. **Finish with Herbs**: Stir in the fresh Thai basil leaves just before serving.

5. **Serve**: Ladle the curry over steamed jasmine rice and enjoy the vibrant flavors.

Cooking Tips:

- **Adjusting Spice Levels**: If you prefer a milder curry, reduce the amount of green curry paste or remove the seeds from the chilies before adding them.
- **Fresh Ingredients:** Use fresh Thai basil instead of regular basil for an authentic flavor. Similarly, fresh kaffir lime leaves add a unique citrus aroma but can be substituted with lime zest if unavailable.
- **Protein Variations**: While chicken is traditional, you can substitute with tofu for a vegetarian version or use shrimp for a seafood twist.

Nutritional Value (Per Serving):
- Calories: 450
- Protein: 28g
- Carbohydrates: 20g
- Fat: 30g
- Fiber: 4g

Recipe 42: Mexican Chiles Rellenos

Serves: 6

Preparation time: 45 minutes

Cooking time: 30 minutes

Category: Entrée

Chiles Rellenos are a staple of Mexican cuisine, embodying the perfect balance of spicy peppers, savory fillings, and a crispy coating. Picture a vibrant Mexican kitchen where the air is filled with the smoky aroma of roasted poblano peppers and the rich scent of cheese melting to perfection. This dish is a delightful combination of flavors and textures, making it a beloved favorite for festive occasions and family dinners alike.

Ingredients:

- 6 large poblano peppers
- 1 cup shredded Monterey Jack cheese
- 1 cup shredded Oaxaca cheese (or mozzarella)
- 3 eggs, separated
- 1 cup all-purpose flour
- 1 tsp salt
- Vegetable oil for frying
- Tomato sauce for serving (optional)

Materials:

- Baking sheet
- Mixing bowls
- Frying pan
- Whisk
- Piping bag (optional)

Procedure:

1. **Roast the Peppers:** Place the poblano peppers directly over a gas flame or under a broiler, turning until the skin is charred and blistered on all sides. Transfer to a bowl, cover with plastic wrap, and let them steam for 15 minutes.
2. **Peel and Seed:** Once cooled, peel off the charred skin, make a small slit on one side, and carefully remove the seeds and membranes.
3. **Stuff the Peppers:** Fill each pepper with a mixture of Monterey Jack and Oaxaca cheese.

4. **Prepare the Batter:** In a bowl, whisk the egg yolks with a pinch of salt. In a separate bowl, beat the egg whites until stiff peaks form.

5. **Combine Eggs:** Gently fold the egg whites into the yolk mixture to create a light batter.

6. **Coat the Peppers:** Lightly dust each stuffed pepper with flour, then dip them into the egg batter, ensuring they are fully coated.

7. **Fry:** Heat vegetable oil in a frying pan over medium heat. Fry the peppers until golden brown on all sides. Drain on paper towels.

8. **Serve:** Serve warm with tomato sauce if desired.

Cooking Tips:

- **Roasting Technique:** For an authentic smoky flavor, roast the peppers over an open flame. If using a broiler, keep a close eye to prevent burning.

- **Cheese Selection:** Combining different cheeses like Monterey Jack and Oaxaca enhances the flavor and melting properties. Ensure the cheese is well-shredded for even distribution.

- **Batter Consistency:** Ensure the egg batter is light and airy by gently folding the egg whites. This will give the Chiles Rellenos a fluffy and crispy exterior.

Nutritional Value (Per Serving):

- Calories: 300
- Protein: 18g
- Carbohydrates: 15g
- Fat: 20g
- Fiber: 4g

Recipe 43: Indian Butter Chicken (Murgh Makhani)

Serves: 4

Preparation time: 20 minutes

Cooking time: 40 minutes

Category: Entrée

Butter Chicken, or Murgh Makhani, is a quintessential dish of Indian cuisine, renowned for its rich, creamy sauce and tender chicken pieces. Originating from the streets of Delhi, this dish has gained global popularity for its harmonious blend of spices, tomatoes, and butter, creating a luxurious sauce that pairs perfectly with naan or basmati rice. Each bite offers a comforting warmth, making it a favorite for both everyday meals and special occasions.

Ingredients:

- 1 lb chicken breast, cubed
- 1 cup plain yogurt
- 1 tbsp garam masala
- 1 tbsp turmeric
- 1 tsp cayenne pepper
- 1 tbsp ground cumin
- 4 tbsp butter
- 1 onion, finely chopped
- 3 garlic cloves, minced
- 1 can (14 oz) tomato puree
- 1/2 cup heavy cream
- 1 tbsp sugar
- Salt to taste
- Fresh cilantro for garnish

Materials:

- Large skillet
- Mixing bowl
- Blender (optional)
- Measuring cups and spoons

Procedure:

1. **Marinate the Chicken:** In a mixing bowl, combine yogurt, garam masala, turmeric, cayenne pepper, and ground cumin. Add the chicken cubes, ensuring they are well-coated. Marinate for at least 30 minutes, preferably overnight for deeper flavor.

2. **Cook the Chicken:** Heat 2 tablespoons of butter in a large skillet over medium heat. Add the marinated chicken and cook until browned and cooked through. Remove and set aside.

3. **Prepare the Sauce:** In the same skillet, melt the remaining 2 tablespoons of butter. Add the chopped onion and sauté until translucent. Stir in the minced garlic and cook for another minute.

4. **Add Tomato Puree:** Pour in the tomato puree, stirring well to combine. Let the mixture simmer for 10 minutes, allowing the flavors to meld. For a smoother sauce, blend the mixture using a blender.

5. **Finish the Dish:** Return the cooked chicken to the skillet. Stir in the heavy cream and sugar, adjusting the seasoning with salt as needed. Let it simmer for an additional 10 minutes.

6. **Serve:** Garnish with fresh cilantro and serve hot with naan or basmati rice.

Cooking Tips:

- **Marination Time:** Allowing the chicken to marinate overnight enhances the depth of flavor and ensures the meat remains tender and juicy.

- **Balancing Flavors:** Adjust the amount of cayenne pepper based on your spice tolerance. The sugar helps balance the acidity of the tomatoes, creating a smooth and rich sauce.
- **Cream Alternatives:** For a lighter version, substitute heavy cream with coconut milk or Greek yogurt. Ensure to add it towards the end to prevent curdling.

Nutritional Value (Per Serving):

- Calories: 500
- Protein: 32g
- Carbohydrates: 15g
- Fat: 35g
- Fiber: 3g

Recipe 44: Spanish Paella

Serves: 4

Preparation time: 15 minutes

Cooking time: 20 minutes

Category: Entrée

Paella is Spain's iconic dish, a vibrant and festive one-pan meal that brings together the freshest seafood, succulent meats, and aromatic saffron-infused rice. Originating from the coastal regions, Paella captures the essence of Spanish gatherings, where friends and family come together to enjoy this colorful and flavorful dish under the warm Mediterranean sun.

Each spoonful is a journey through Spain's rich culinary landscape, celebrating tradition and communal dining.

Ingredients:

- 2 cups bomba or arborio rice
- 1 lb mixed seafood (shrimp, mussels, calamari)
- 1/2 lb chicken thighs, diced
- 1 chorizo sausage, sliced
- 1 onion, finely chopped
- 1 red bell pepper, sliced
- 3 cloves garlic, minced
- 1 can (14 oz) diced tomatoes
- 4 cups chicken or seafood broth
- 1 tsp saffron threads
- 1 tsp smoked paprika
- 1 cup frozen peas
- 2 tbsp olive oil
- Lemon wedges for serving
- Fresh parsley, chopped for garnish

Materials:

- Large paella pan or wide, shallow skillet
- Wooden spoon
- Measuring cups and spoons

Procedure:

1. **Prepare the Broth:** Warm the chicken or seafood broth in a saucepan and infuse with saffron threads. Keep it warm on low heat.

2. **Cook the Meats:** In the paella pan, heat olive oil over medium heat. Add the diced chicken and chorizo slices, cooking until browned. Remove and set aside.

3. **Sauté the Vegetables:** In the same pan, add the chopped onion and red bell pepper. Sauté until softened. Add the minced garlic and cook for another minute.

4. **Add Rice and Spices:** Stir in the rice, ensuring it's well-coated with the oil and vegetables. Sprinkle in the smoked paprika and mix thoroughly.

5. **Incorporate Liquids:** Pour in the diced tomatoes and the saffron-infused broth. Bring to a simmer and let it cook uncovered for about 15 minutes, stirring occasionally.

6. **Add Seafood and Peas:** Return the browned chicken and chorizo to the pan. Add the mixed seafood and frozen peas. Continue to simmer without stirring until the rice is cooked and the seafood is done, about 10-15 minutes.

7. **Rest and Serve:** Remove the pan from heat and let it rest for 5 minutes. Garnish with fresh parsley and serve with lemon wedges.

Cooking Tips:

- **Rice Selection:** Use short-grain rice like bomba or arborio, which absorbs liquid well without becoming mushy, ensuring a perfect texture.

- **Saffron Quality:** Invest in high-quality saffron for authentic flavor and vibrant color. Soak the threads in warm broth to release their full aroma.
- **Avoid Stirring:** Once the rice and liquids are combined, avoid stirring the paella. This helps develop the coveted socarrat, the crispy bottom layer of rice.

Nutritional Value (Per Serving):

- Calories: 550
- Protein: 35g
- Carbohydrates: 60g
- Fat: 20g
- Fiber: 5g

Recipe 45: Moroccan Lamb Tagine

Serves: 4
Preparation time: 20 minutes
Cooking time: 2 hours
Category: Entrée

Moroccan Lamb Tagine is a fragrant and hearty dish that embodies the rich culinary traditions of North Africa. Slow-cooked to perfection, the tender lamb melds with an array of spices, dried fruits, and vegetables, creating a harmonious blend of sweet and savory flavors. Imagine the bustling souks of Marrakech, where the air is filled with the scent of cumin, coriander, and cinnamon, inviting you to savor this exquisite and comforting meal.

Ingredients:

- 2 lbs lamb shoulder, cut into chunks
- 2 onions, finely chopped
- 3 garlic cloves, minced
- 2 carrots, sliced
- 1 sweet potato, cubed
- 1 can (14 oz) chickpeas, drained and rinsed
- 1/2 cup dried apricots, halved
- 1/4 cup raisins
- 2 tbsp tomato paste
- 4 cups beef or lamb broth
- 2 tbsp olive oil
- 1 tsp ground cumin
- 1 tsp ground coriander
- 1 tsp ground cinnamon
- 1/2 tsp ground turmeric
- 1/2 tsp ground ginger
- Salt and pepper to taste
- Fresh cilantro for garnish

Materials:

- Tagine pot or Dutch oven
- Wooden spoon
- Measuring cups and spoons

Procedure:

1. **Brown the Lamb:** Heat olive oil in a tagine or Dutch oven over medium-high heat. Add the lamb chunks and brown them on all sides. Remove and set aside.

2. **Sauté Aromatics:** In the same pot, add the chopped onions and sauté until translucent. Add the minced garlic and cook for another minute.

3. **Add Spices:** Stir in the ground cumin, coriander, cinnamon, turmeric, and ginger. Cook for 2 minutes to release the spices' aromas.

4. **Incorporate Tomato Paste:** Add the tomato paste and mix well to coat the onions and spices.

5. **Combine Ingredients:** Return the browned lamb to the pot. Add the carrots, sweet potatoes, chickpeas, dried apricots, and raisins. Pour in the beef or lamb broth, ensuring the ingredients are just covered.

6. **Simmer:** Bring the mixture to a boil, then reduce the heat to low. Cover and let it simmer for 1.5 to 2 hours, or until the lamb is tender and the flavors have melded.

7. **Adjust Seasoning:** Season with salt and pepper to taste. If the sauce is too thick, add a bit more broth or water.

8. **Serve:** Garnish with fresh cilantro and serve hot with couscous or crusty bread.

Cooking Tips:

- **Slow Cooking:** For the most tender lamb, cook the tagine on low heat for an extended period. Alternatively, use a slow cooker set to low for 6-8 hours.
- **Balancing Flavors:** The sweetness from dried apricots and raisins balances the warm spices. Adjust the amount based on your preference for sweetness.
- **Layering Spices:** Toasting the spices briefly before adding liquids enhances their flavors, making the tagine more aromatic and flavorful.

Nutritional Value (Per Serving):

- Calories: 600
- Protein: 35g
- Carbohydrates: 50g
- Fat: 25g
- Fiber: 8g

Recipe 46: Greek Moussaka

Serves: 6

Preparation time: 45 minutes

Cooking time: 1 hour 30 minutes

Category: Main Course

Transport yourself to a sun-kissed Greek island, where every meal is a celebration of flavors. Moussaka is a rich, layered dish combining spiced meat, eggplant, and creamy béchamel sauce. This recipe is as comforting as a Mediterranean sunset, with every bite telling a story of tradition and warmth.

Ingredients:

- 2 large eggplants, sliced
- 1 lb ground lamb or beef
- 1 onion, finely chopped
- 2 cloves garlic, minced
- 1 can (14 oz) diced tomatoes
- 1 tsp ground cinnamon
- 1/2 tsp ground allspice
- 1/4 cup red wine
- 1 cup béchamel sauce
- 1/2 cup grated Parmesan cheese
- Olive oil for frying
- Salt and pepper to taste

Materials:

- Large skillet
- Baking dish

Procedure:

1. **Prepare the Eggplant:** Sprinkle the eggplant slices with salt and let them sit for 30 minutes to draw out moisture. Pat dry and fry in olive oil until golden. Set aside.
2. **Cook the Meat:** In a skillet, sauté onions and garlic in olive oil. Add ground lamb, cook until browned, then stir in tomatoes, cinnamon, allspice, and red wine. Simmer for 15 minutes.

3. **Layer the Moussaka:** In a baking dish, layer eggplant slices, followed by the meat mixture. Pour béchamel sauce on top and sprinkle with Parmesan.
4. **Bake:** Bake in a preheated oven at 350°F for 30-40 minutes until golden and bubbly.

Cooking Tip: For a lighter version, you can grill the eggplant instead of frying. Let the moussaka rest for 10 minutes before serving to allow the flavors to meld.

Nutritional Value (Per Serving):

- Calories: 450
- Protein: 24g
- Carbohydrates: 22g
- Fat: 30g
- Fiber: 7g

Recipe 47: Brazilian Feijoada

Serves: 8-10

Preparation time: 30 minutes

Cooking time: 2 hours 30 minute

Category: Main Course

Feijoada is Brazil's national dish, a hearty black bean stew infused with smoky meats and vibrant spices. Imagine yourself at a Brazilian family gathering, where this flavorful stew is always at the center of the table. Traditionally served with rice, collard greens, and orange slices, this dish is all about comfort and celebration.

Ingredients:

- 1 lb black beans (soaked overnight)
- 1 lb pork shoulder, cubed
- 1 lb smoked sausage, sliced
- 2 strips bacon, chopped
- 1 onion, diced
- 3 cloves garlic, minced
- 2 bay leaves
- 1 tbsp paprika
- 1 tbsp olive oil
- Salt and pepper to taste
- Fresh cilantro for garnish

Materials:

- Large pot or Dutch oven
- Stirring spoon

Procedure:

1. **Cook the Meat:** In a large pot, heat olive oil and cook bacon until crispy. Add pork shoulder and sausage, browning them on all sides.
2. **Add Aromatics:** Stir in onions, garlic, bay leaves, and paprika, cooking until the onions are soft.

3. **Simmer with Beans:** Drain the soaked beans and add them to the pot. Cover with water and simmer for 2-3 hours until the beans and meat are tender.

4. **Serve:** Serve hot, garnished with fresh cilantro and accompanied by rice, collard greens, and orange slices.

Cooking Tip: For a deeper flavor, cook the feijoada the day before and reheat it before serving. The flavors develop beautifully overnight.

Nutritional Value (Per Serving):

- Calories: 550
- Protein: 35g
- Carbohydrates: 35g
- Fat: 28g
- Fiber: 12g

Recipe 48: Thai Green Curry

Serves: 4

Preparation time: 15 minutes

Cooking time: 20 minutes

Category: Main Course

Imagine a bustling Thai street market, where the aroma of fragrant herbs fills the air. Thai Green Curry is an aromatic blend of lemongrass, ginger, and green chilies, balanced with the creamy richness of coconut milk. This dish brings the flavors of Thailand to your kitchen in one delicious, easy-to-make curry.

Ingredients:

- 1 lb chicken breast, sliced
- 2 tbsp Thai green curry paste
- 1 can (14 oz) coconut milk
- 1 cup chicken broth
- 1 bell pepper, sliced
- 1 zucchini, sliced
- 1 cup bamboo shoots
- 2 tbsp fish sauce
- 1 tbsp brown sugar
- Fresh basil for garnish

Materials:

- Large saucepan
- Stirring spoon

Procedure:

1. **Cook the Curry Paste:** In a large saucepan, sauté the green curry paste in oil for 2-3 minutes until fragrant.
2. **Add Chicken and Vegetables:** Stir in chicken and vegetables, cooking until the chicken is browned and vegetables are tender.
3. **Simmer:** Add coconut milk, chicken broth, fish sauce, and brown sugar. Simmer for 10-15 minutes.

4. **Serve:** Garnish with fresh basil and serve with steamed jasmine rice.

Cooking Tip: For an extra burst of flavor, squeeze fresh lime juice into the curry before serving.

Nutritional Value (Per Serving):

- Calories: 400
- Protein: 30g
- Carbohydrates: 15g
- Fat: 28g
- Fiber: 4g

Recipe 49: Italian Caprese Salad

Serves: 4

Preparation time: 10 minutes

Category: Appetizer

Close your eyes and picture a sun-drenched Italian terrace. Caprese salad, with its vibrant colors and fresh flavors, captures the essence of Italian simplicity. The perfect combination of ripe tomatoes, creamy mozzarella, and fragrant basil is a true celebration of freshness.

Ingredients:

- 2 large ripe tomatoes, sliced
- 8 oz fresh mozzarella, sliced
- 1 bunch fresh basil leaves
- 2 tbsp olive oil
- 1 tbsp balsamic glaze
- Salt and pepper to taste

Materials:

- Serving plate
- Knife

Procedure:

1. **Assemble the Salad:** Alternate slices of tomato and mozzarella on a serving plate, tucking fresh basil leaves in between.
2. **Drizzle with Olive Oil and Glaze:** Drizzle with olive oil and balsamic glaze, then season with salt and pepper.

3. **Serve Fresh:** Serve immediately to enjoy the fresh flavors.

Cooking Tip: For the best flavor, use ripe, in-season tomatoes and high-quality olive oil. Adding a sprinkle of sea salt enhances the dish.

Nutritional Value (Per Serving):

- Calories: 250
- Protein: 12g
- Carbohydrates: 8g
- Fat: 20g
- Fiber: 2g

Recipe 50: Indian Butter Chicken (Murgh Makhani)

Serves: 4

Preparation time: 20 minutes

Cooking time: 30 minutes

Category: Main Course

Imagine yourself wandering through the bustling streets of Delhi, where the vibrant colors and aromatic spices fill the air. Butter Chicken, or Murgh Makhani, is the ultimate indulgence in Indian cuisine—a luxurious, creamy curry that captures the essence of comfort and flavor in every bite. This dish combines tender chicken with a velvety tomato and cream sauce, perfect for a cozy dinner or impressing guests at your next gathering.

Ingredients:

- 1 lb boneless chicken thighs, cut into bite-sized pieces
- 1/2 cup plain yogurt
- 2 tbsp garam masala
- 1 tbsp turmeric powder
- 1 tbsp paprika
- 2 tbsp butter
- 1 large onion, finely chopped
- 3 cloves garlic, minced
- 1 tbsp ginger, minced
- 1 can (14 oz) tomato puree
- 1 cup heavy cream
- 1 tsp chili powder (adjust to taste)
- Salt to taste

- Fresh cilantro for garnish

Materials:

- Large skillet or Dutch oven
- Mixing bowl
- Stirring spoon

Procedure:

1. **Marinate the Chicken:** In a mixing bowl, combine yogurt, garam masala, turmeric, and paprika. Add the chicken pieces and marinate for at least 30 minutes, or preferably overnight for maximum flavor.
2. **Cook the Chicken:** Heat butter in a large skillet or Dutch oven over medium heat. Add the chopped onions and cook until golden brown. Stir in garlic and ginger, cooking until fragrant.
3. **Add Chicken:** Add the marinated chicken to the skillet, cooking until the chicken is browned on all sides and cooked through.
4. **Prepare the Sauce:** Pour in tomato puree, chili powder, and a pinch of salt. Simmer for 10-15 minutes, allowing the flavors to meld.
5. **Finish with Cream:** Stir in the heavy cream and cook for an additional 5 minutes until the sauce is creamy and well-combined.
6. **Garnish and Serve:** Garnish with fresh cilantro and serve hot with basmati rice or naan bread.

Cooking Tip: For an extra layer of flavor, roast the chicken in the oven at 400°F for about 20 minutes before adding it to the sauce. This will give the chicken a slightly charred, smoky taste that enhances the overall dish.

Nutritional Value (Per Serving):

- Calories: 450
- Protein: 30g
- Carbohydrates: 10g
- Fat: 32g
- Fiber: 2g

Recipe 51: Mexican Chiles Rellenos

Serves: 4

Preparation time: 30 minutes

Cooking time: 30 minute

Category: Main Course

Step into the vibrant world of Mexican cuisine with Chiles Rellenos—a classic dish that beautifully showcases the rich flavors and traditions of Mexico. Imagine biting into a perfectly roasted poblano pepper, filled with a savory blend of cheese and spices, then enveloped in a crispy batter and fried to golden perfection. This dish is a celebration of textures and tastes, bringing together the smokiness of the peppers with the gooey goodness of melted cheese.

Ingredients:

- 6 large poblano peppers
- 1 cup shredded cheese (cheddar, Monterey Jack, or a blend)
- 1/2 cup cooked ground beef or chorizo (optional)
- 1/2 cup flour
- 3 large eggs, separated
- 1/2 tsp baking powder
- Salt and pepper to taste
- Vegetable oil for frying
- Tomato sauce for serving (optional)

Materials:

- Baking sheet
- Skillet
- Mixing bowls
- Paper towels
- Whisk
- Tongs

Procedure:

1. **Prepare the Peppers:** Preheat your oven to 400°F (200°C). Place the poblano peppers on a baking sheet and roast for 20-25 minutes, turning occasionally, until the skins are blistered and charred. Remove from the oven and place in a plastic bag or covered bowl to steam for 10 minutes. Once cool, peel off the skins and remove the seeds and membranes carefully.

2. **Stuff the Peppers:** Stuff each pepper with shredded cheese and, if using, a spoonful of cooked ground beef or chorizo. Gently press the opening to seal the filling inside.

3. **Prepare the Batter:** In a mixing bowl, whisk the egg yolks with flour, baking powder, salt, and pepper until smooth. In another bowl, beat the egg whites until stiff peaks form. Gently fold the egg whites into the yolk mixture until combined.

4. **Fry the Peppers:** Heat vegetable oil in a skillet over medium heat. Dip each stuffed pepper into the batter, coating it thoroughly. Carefully place the peppers in the hot oil and fry for 3-4 minutes on each side, or until golden brown and crispy. Remove and drain on paper towels.

5. **Serve:** Serve the Chiles Rellenos hot with a side of tomato sauce, if desired.

Cooking Tip: For extra flavor, add a pinch of cumin or paprika to the cheese filling. If you prefer a lighter version, you can bake the stuffed peppers instead of frying them. Place the battered peppers on a baking sheet and bake at 375°F (190°C) for 20-25 minutes, or until golden and crispy.

Nutritional Value (Per Serving):

- Calories: 350
- Protein: 18g
- Carbohydrates: 20g
- Fat: 22g
- Fiber: 4g

Recipe 52: Japanese Chicken Teriyaki

Serves: 4

Preparation time: 10 minutes

Marinating time: 30 minutes

Cooking time: 15 minutes

Category: Main Course

Transport yourself to the bustling streets of Tokyo with this classic Japanese Chicken Teriyaki. Picture a succulent chicken breast glazed with a glossy, sweet-savory teriyaki sauce, served over a bed of fluffy rice. This dish combines the umami depth of soy sauce with the caramelized sweetness of mirin, creating a harmonious balance of flavors that's both comforting and delicious. Perfect for a weeknight dinner or impressing guests with your culinary skills!

Ingredients:

- 4 boneless, skinless chicken breasts
- 1/4 cup soy sauce
- 1/4 cup mirin (sweet rice wine)

- 2 tbsp honey or brown sugar
- 2 tbsp rice vinegar
- 2 cloves garlic, minced
- 1 tsp fresh ginger, minced
- 1 tbsp vegetable oil
- 1 tbsp cornstarch mixed with 2 tbsp water (for thickening)
- 1 tbsp sesame seeds (for garnish)
- 2 green onions, sliced (for garnish)
- Cooked white rice (for serving)

Materials:

- Skillet or grill pan
- Small saucepan
- Mixing bowl
- Whisk
- Tongs

Procedure:

1. **Prepare the Sauce:** In a small saucepan, combine soy sauce, mirin, honey, rice vinegar, garlic, and ginger. Bring to a simmer over medium heat, whisking occasionally. Once the mixture has slightly reduced, stir in the cornstarch mixture to thicken the sauce. Remove from heat and set aside.

2. **Cook the Chicken:** Heat vegetable oil in a skillet or grill pan over medium-high heat. Season the chicken breasts with salt and pepper. Cook the chicken for 5-7 minutes on each side, or until fully cooked

and golden brown. The internal temperature should reach 165°F (75°C).

3. **Glaze the Chicken:** Once the chicken is cooked, pour the teriyaki sauce over the chicken in the skillet. Let it simmer for a few minutes, allowing the sauce to glaze the chicken and caramelize slightly.

4. **Serve:** Slice the glazed chicken and serve over cooked white rice. Garnish with sesame seeds and sliced green onions.

Cooking Tip: For an extra layer of flavor, marinate the chicken in a portion of the teriyaki sauce for 30 minutes before cooking. If you prefer a more intense flavor, let the sauce reduce further on the stove until it reaches a thicker consistency. Serve with steamed vegetables for a complete meal.

Nutritional Value (Per Serving):

- Calories: 300
- Protein: 27g
- Carbohydrates: 20g
- Fat: 10g
- Fiber: 1g

Recipe 53: Greek Spanakopita (Spinach and Feta Pie)

Serves: 8
Preparation time: 30 minutes
Cooking time: 45 minutes

Imagine the sun-drenched landscapes of Greece, where fresh, vibrant flavors come together in a flaky, golden pastry. This Greek Spanakopita is a celebration of Greek culinary traditions, featuring layers of crisp phyllo dough filled with a rich, savory mixture of spinach and feta. Each bite offers a delightful contrast between the buttery crunch of the phyllo and the creamy, herb-infused filling. Perfect as a starter or a light main course, Spanakopita embodies the essence of Mediterranean comfort food.

Ingredients:

- 1 package phyllo dough (16 oz), thawed
- 2 tbsp olive oil
- 1 large onion, finely chopped
- 3 cloves garlic, minced
- 1 lb fresh spinach, washed and chopped (or 1 package frozen spinach, thawed and drained)
- 1 cup feta cheese, crumbled
- 1/2 cup ricotta cheese
- 2 large eggs, beaten
- 1/4 cup fresh dill, chopped (or 1 tbsp dried dill)
- 1/4 cup fresh parsley, chopped
- Salt and pepper to taste
- 2 tbsp melted butter (for brushing)

Materials:

- Large skillet
- Mixing bowl
- 9x13-inch baking dish
- Pastry brush

Procedure:

1. **Prepare the Filling:** Heat olive oil in a large skillet over medium heat. Sauté the onion and garlic until softened and translucent. Add the spinach and cook until wilted and any excess moisture has evaporated. Transfer the mixture to a mixing bowl and let it cool slightly.

2. **Mix the Filling:** Once the spinach mixture has cooled, stir in feta cheese, ricotta cheese, beaten eggs, dill, parsley, salt, and pepper until well combined.

3. **Assemble the Pie:** Preheat your oven to 375°F (190°C). Brush a 9x13-inch baking dish with melted butter. Lay a sheet of phyllo dough in the dish, brushing it lightly with butter. Repeat layering with half of the phyllo sheets, brushing each layer with butter.

4. **Add the Filling:** Spread the spinach and feta mixture evenly over the phyllo layers. Top with the remaining phyllo sheets, continuing to brush each layer with butter.

5. **Bake:** Trim any overhanging phyllo and tuck the edges into the dish. Brush the top layer of phyllo with butter and score the top into squares with a knife. Bake for 30-40 minutes, or until the phyllo is golden brown and crispy.

6. **Cool and Serve:** Allow the Spanakopita to cool for a few minutes before cutting into squares. Serve warm or at room temperature.

Cooking Tip: To ensure a crispy, non-soggy bottom, make sure to drain excess moisture from the spinach thoroughly. If using frozen spinach, squeeze out as much liquid as possible before mixing with the other ingredients. For added texture, consider sprinkling sesame seeds on top before baking.

Nutritional Value (Per Serving):

- Calories: 280
- Protein: 10g
- Carbohydrates: 22g
- Fat: 18g
- Fiber: 2g

Recipe 54: Thai Mango Sticky Rice

Serves: 4

Preparation time: 15 minutes

Cooking time: 30 minutes

Category: Dessert

A trip to Thailand is not complete without savoring Mango Sticky Rice. This quintessential Thai dessert combines creamy, sweet coconut milk-infused sticky rice with ripe, juicy mangoes. Imagine enjoying this delectable treat on a warm evening, with the tropical flavors melting in your mouth. It's a perfect blend of texture and taste, offering a sweet escape to the heart of Thailand with every bite.

Ingredients:

- 1 cup sticky rice (glutinous rice)
- 1 1/2 cups coconut milk
- 1/2 cup sugar
- 1/4 tsp salt
- 2 ripe mangoes, peeled and sliced
- Sesame seeds or toasted coconut flakes (for garnish, optional)

Materials:

- Medium saucepan
- Steamer basket or bamboo steamer
- Mixing bowl

Procedure:

1. **Prepare the Rice:** Rinse the sticky rice under cold water until the water runs clear. Soak the rice in water for at least 1 hour, or overnight for best results.
2. **Cook the Rice:** Drain the rice and place it in a steamer basket lined with cheesecloth. Steam over simmering water for about 30-40 minutes, or until the rice is tender and sticky.
3. **Make the Coconut Sauce:** While the rice is steaming, combine coconut milk, sugar, and salt in a medium saucepan. Heat over medium heat until the sugar is dissolved, but do not let it boil. Remove from heat.

4. **Mix the Rice and Sauce:** Once the rice is cooked, transfer it to a mixing bowl and pour about 1 cup of the coconut milk mixture over it. Stir to combine and let it sit for about 15 minutes, allowing the rice to absorb the flavors.

5. **Serve:** Spoon the sticky rice onto plates, top with fresh mango slices, and drizzle with additional coconut milk sauce. Garnish with sesame seeds or toasted coconut flakes if desired.

Cooking Tip: For the best texture, use Thai sticky rice (also known as glutinous rice) and avoid substituting with regular rice. To ensure the rice is perfectly sticky, soak it thoroughly and steam it rather than boiling it.

Nutritional Value (Per Serving):

- Calories: 320
- Protein: 3g
- Carbohydrates: 70g
- Fat: 8g
- Fiber: 2g

Recipe 55: Mexican Tres Leches Cake

Serves: 12

Preparation time: 20 minutes

Baking time: 30 minutes

Chilling time: 4 hours

Category: Dessert

Tres Leches Cake, a beloved Mexican dessert, is a decadent sponge cake soaked in a rich mixture of three types of milk. This indulgent treat offers a moist and creamy texture, perfect for celebrations or a sweet end to any meal. Picture yourself cutting into this cake, its velvety, milky layers oozing with flavor, creating a truly satisfying dessert experience.

Ingredients:

- **For the Cake:**
  - 1 cup all-purpose flour
  - 1 1/2 tsp baking powder
  - 1/4 tsp salt
  - 1/2 cup unsalted butter, softened
  - 1 cup sugar
  - 4 large eggs
  - 1 tsp vanilla extract
  - 1/2 cup milk
- **For the Milk Mixture:**
  - 1 can (14 oz) sweetened condensed milk
  - 1 can (12 oz) evaporated milk
  - 1/2 cup whole milk
- **For the Topping:**
  - 1 cup heavy cream
  - 2 tbsp sugar
  - Fresh berries (optional, for garnish)

Materials:

- 9x13-inch baking dish
- Mixing bowls
- Electric mixer
- Whisk

Procedure:

1. **Prepare the Cake:** Preheat your oven to 350°F (175°C). Grease and flour a 9x13-inch baking dish. In a medium bowl, whisk together flour, baking powder, and salt. In a large bowl, cream the butter and sugar until light and fluffy. Add eggs one at a time, beating well after each addition. Mix in vanilla extract. Gradually add flour mixture to the butter mixture, alternating with milk, until well combined.

2. **Bake the Cake:** Pour the batter into the prepared baking dish and bake for 25-30 minutes, or until a toothpick inserted into the center comes out clean. Allow the cake to cool completely in the dish.

3. **Prepare the Milk Mixture:** In a bowl, whisk together sweetened condensed milk, evaporated milk, and whole milk.

4. **Soak the Cake:** Once the cake is cool, poke holes all over the surface with a fork. Pour the milk mixture evenly over the cake, allowing it to soak in.

5. **Prepare the Topping:** In a medium bowl, whip the heavy cream and sugar until soft peaks form. Spread the whipped cream over the soaked cake and garnish with fresh berries if desired.

Cooking Tip: To ensure the cake soaks up the milk mixture evenly, poke the cake with a fork to create more holes. Allow the cake to soak for at least a few hours or overnight for the best flavor and texture.

Nutritional Value (Per Serving):

- Calories: 350
- Protein: 6g
- Carbohydrates: 45g
- Fat: 17g
- Fiber: 1g

Recipe 56: Korean Bulgogi

Serves: 4

Preparation time: 15 minutes

Marinating time: 1-2 hours

Cooking time: 10 minutes

Category: Main Course

Korean Bulgogi, or marinated beef, is a dish that bursts with umami flavors and tender textures. Imagine the sizzling sound of marinated beef grilling to perfection, filling the air with a sweet and savory aroma. This dish is a staple in Korean cuisine, offering a mouthwatering combination of flavors that will transport you straight to a bustling Korean BBQ.

Ingredients:

- 1 lb beef sirloin, thinly sliced
- 1/4 cup soy sauce
- 2 tbsp brown sugar
- 2 tbsp sesame oil
- 3 cloves garlic, minced
- 1 tbsp ginger, grated
- 1/4 cup green onions, chopped
- 1 tbsp rice vinegar
- 1 tbsp sesame seeds
- 1/2 tsp black pepper
- 1 small carrot, julienned
- 1/2 onion, thinly sliced
- 1 tbsp vegetable oil (for cooking)

Materials:

- Mixing bowl
- Grill or skillet
- Tongs

Procedure:

1. **Marinate the Beef:** In a mixing bowl, combine soy sauce, brown sugar, sesame oil, garlic, ginger, green onions, rice vinegar, sesame seeds, and black pepper. Add the sliced beef and mix well. Let it marinate for at least 30 minutes, or overnight for deeper flavor.
2. **Cook the Beef:** Heat vegetable oil in a grill or skillet over medium-high heat. Add the marinated beef, carrots, and onions. Cook for 5-7 minutes, or until the beef is cooked through and slightly caramelized.
3. **Serve:** Transfer the cooked beef to a serving platter and garnish with additional sesame seeds if desired. Serve with steamed rice and your favorite Korean side dishes.

Cooking Tip: For the most tender Bulgogi, slice the beef thinly against the grain. If you have time, marinate the beef overnight to enhance the flavors. Use a hot grill or skillet to achieve a nice caramelization on the beef.

Nutritional Value (Per Serving):

- Calories: 300
- Protein: 23g

- Carbohydrates: 15g
- Fat: 16g
- Fiber: 2g

Recipe 57: Italian Caprese Salad

Serves: 4

Preparation time: 10 minutes

Category: Main Course

Indian Butter Chicken, or Murgh Makhani, is a rich and creamy dish beloved around the world. Imagine savoring tender chicken pieces enveloped in a velvety tomato and butter sauce, with warm spices that create a symphony of flavors. This dish, with its deep, aromatic spices and creamy sauce, is a true comfort food that will make your taste buds dance.

Ingredients:

- 1 lb boneless chicken thighs, cut into bite-sized pieces
- 2 tbsp vegetable oil
- 1 large onion, finely chopped
- 3 cloves garlic, minced
- 1 tbsp ginger, grated
- 1 can (14 oz) tomato puree
- 1/2 cup heavy cream
- 1/4 cup plain yogurt
- 2 tbsp butter

- 1 tbsp garam masala
- 1 tsp ground cumin
- 1/2 tsp turmeric
- 1/2 tsp paprika
- 1/2 tsp chili powder
- Salt to taste
- Fresh cilantro, chopped (for garnish)

Materials:

- Large skillet or pan
- Mixing bowl
- Knife

Procedure:

1. **Marinate the Chicken:** In a bowl, combine chicken pieces with yogurt, a pinch of salt, and 1/2 teaspoon of chili powder. Marinate for at least 30 minutes.

2. **Cook the Chicken:** Heat vegetable oil in a large skillet over medium heat. Add onions and cook until softened. Add garlic and ginger, cooking for another minute. Stir in the marinated chicken and cook until browned and cooked through.

3. **Prepare the Sauce:** Add tomato puree, garam masala, cumin, turmeric, paprika, and remaining chili powder. Stir well and let it simmer for 10 minutes.

4. **Finish the Dish:** Stir in heavy cream and butter. Simmer for an additional 5 minutes, allowing the flavors to meld.

5. **Garnish and Serve:** Garnish with fresh cilantro and serve with steamed rice or naan bread.

Cooking Tip: For the best flavor, marinate the chicken overnight. Adjust the spice levels to your preference and serve with a side of basmati rice or naan to soak up the rich sauce.

Nutritional Value (Per Serving):

- Calories: 400
- Protein: 30g
- Carbohydrates: 15g
- Fat: 25g
- Fiber: 2g

Recipe 58: Indian Butter Chicken

Serves: 4

Preparation time: 20 minutes

Marinating time: 1 hour

Cooking time: 30 minutes

Category: Main Course

Indian Butter Chicken, or Murgh Makhani, is a rich and creamy dish beloved around the world. Imagine savoring tender chicken pieces enveloped in a velvety tomato and butter sauce, with warm spices that create a symphony of flavors. This dish, with its deep, aromatic spices and creamy sauce, is a true comfort food that will make your taste buds dance.

Ingredients:

- 1 lb boneless chicken thighs, cut into bite-sized pieces
- 2 tbsp vegetable oil
- 1 large onion, finely chopped
- 3 cloves garlic, minced
- 1 tbsp ginger, grated
- 1 can (14 oz) tomato puree
- 1/2 cup heavy cream
- 1/4 cup plain yogurt
- 2 tbsp butter
- 1 tbsp garam masala
- 1 tsp ground cumin
- 1/2 tsp turmeric
- 1/2 tsp paprika
- 1/2 tsp chili powder
- Salt to taste
- Fresh cilantro, chopped (for garnish)

Materials:

- Large skillet or pan
- Mixing bowl
- Knife

Procedure:

1. **Marinate the Chicken:** In a bowl, combine chicken pieces with yogurt, a pinch of salt, and 1/2 teaspoon of chili powder. Marinate for at least 30 minutes.
2. **Cook the Chicken:** Heat vegetable oil in a large skillet over medium heat. Add onions and cook until softened. Add garlic and ginger, cooking for another minute. Stir in the marinated chicken and cook until browned and cooked through.
3. **Prepare the Sauce:** Add tomato puree, garam masala, cumin, turmeric, paprika, and remaining chili powder. Stir well and let it simmer for 10 minutes.
4. **Finish the Dish:** Stir in heavy cream and butter. Simmer for an additional 5 minutes, allowing the flavors to meld.
5. **Garnish and Serve:** Garnish with fresh cilantro and serve with steamed rice or naan bread.

Cooking Tip: For the best flavor, marinate the chicken overnight. Adjust the spice levels to your preference and serve with a side of basmati rice or naan to soak up the rich sauce.

Nutritional Value (Per Serving):

- Calories: 400

- Protein: 30g
- Carbohydrates: 15g
- Fat: 25g
- Fiber: 2g

Recipe 59: Japanese Miso Soup

Serves: 4

Preparation time: 10 minutes

Cooking time: 15 minutes

Category: Soup

Japanese Miso Soup is a warm, comforting dish that embodies the subtle elegance of Japanese cuisine. Picture yourself cozying up with a steaming bowl of miso soup, where each spoonful delivers a harmonious blend of umami flavors and nourishing ingredients. This simple yet satisfying soup is a staple in Japanese meals, offering both comfort and a taste of tradition.

Ingredients:

- 4 cups dashi broth (or water)
- 3 tbsp miso paste (white or red)
- 1/2 cup tofu, cubed
- 1/4 cup green onions, chopped
- 1/4 cup wakame seaweed (rehydrated if dried)

Materials:

- Medium saucepan

- Whisk
- Ladle

Procedure:

1. **Prepare the Broth:** Heat dashi broth in a saucepan over medium heat until it's warm but not boiling.
2. **Dissolve the Miso:** In a small bowl, mix miso paste with a ladleful of hot broth until smooth. Stir this mixture back into the saucepan with the remaining broth.
3. **Add Tofu and Seaweed:** Gently add cubed tofu and wakame seaweed to the soup. Heat until the tofu is warmed through, being careful not to boil the soup.
4. **Garnish and Serve:** Stir in chopped green onions and serve hot.

Cooking Tip: Avoid boiling the miso paste to maintain its delicate flavors. For an added touch, experiment with different types of miso paste or add mushrooms and vegetables to customize the soup.

Nutritional Value (Per Serving):

- Calories: 80
- Protein: 6g
- Carbohydrates: 8g
- Fat: 3g
- Fiber: 1g

Recipe 60: Greek Spanakopita

Serves: 8

Preparation time: 30 minutes

Cooking time: 45 minutes

Category: Main Course

Spanakopita, a classic Greek pie, is a savory delight that brings together spinach, feta cheese, and flaky phyllo pastry. Imagine a warm, golden-brown pie filled with a luscious mixture of spinach and feta, each bite offering a crispy texture and rich flavor. This dish, often enjoyed as a hearty appetizer or main course, perfectly embodies the essence of Greek cuisine.

Ingredients:

- 1 lb fresh spinach, washed and chopped
- 1/2 cup feta cheese, crumbled
- 1/2 cup ricotta cheese
- 1/4 cup grated Parmesan cheese
- 1/2 cup onion, finely chopped
- 2 cloves garlic, minced
- 1/4 cup fresh dill, chopped
- 1/4 cup fresh parsley, chopped
- 1/4 cup olive oil
- 10 sheets phyllo dough
- 1 large egg, beaten (for brushing)

Materials:

- Large mixing bowl
- 9x13-inch baking dish
- Pastry brush

Procedure:

1. **Prepare the Filling:** In a large skillet, heat olive oil over medium heat. Add onions and garlic, cooking until softened. Stir in spinach and cook until wilted. Transfer to a large bowl and let cool slightly. Mix in feta, ricotta, Parmesan, dill, and parsley.

2. **Assemble the Pie:** Preheat your oven to 375°F (190°C). Lightly grease a 9x13-inch baking dish. Layer 5 sheets of phyllo dough in the dish, brushing each sheet with olive oil. Spread the spinach mixture evenly over the phyllo. Top with remaining phyllo sheets, brushing each sheet with olive oil. Brush the top layer with beaten egg.

3. **Bake the Pie:** Bake for 35-40 minutes, or until the phyllo is golden brown and crispy. Allow to cool slightly before cutting into squares.

Cooking Tip: Handle phyllo dough with care, as it can dry out quickly. Keep unused sheets covered with a damp towel to prevent drying. For a richer filling, add sautéed mushrooms or sun-dried tomatoes.

Nutritional Value (Per Serving):

- Calories: 280
- Protein: 10g
- Carbohydrates: 25g
- Fat: 15g
- Fiber: 3g

Recipe 61: Avocado Toast with a Twist

Preparation Time: 15 minutes

Cooking Time: None

Total Time: 15 minutes

Category: Appetizer

Ah, the classic avocado toast. But we're not stopping at the basics here—no, we're giving this staple a twist that'll make your taste buds tango. Picture yourself on a sun-dappled patio, sipping on a morning espresso, the aroma of toasted bread wafting through the air. Life is good, but it's about to get even better with this recipe.

- **Ingredients:**
- 1 ripe avocado
- 1 slice whole-grain bread
- 1 tsp lemon juice
- 1 tbsp feta cheese, crumbled
- 1 tbsp pomegranate seeds
- Pinch of chili flakes
- Salt and pepper to taste

Materials:
- Toaster
- Fork
- Knife
- Small bowl

Procedure:
1. Pop that slice of bread into the toaster and let it do its thing—golden, crispy perfection is the goal.
2. While the bread toasts, halve your avocado and scoop the flesh into a small bowl.
3. Add lemon juice, salt, and pepper to the avocado, then mash it up with a fork. Keep it chunky—you're not making guac.
4. Spread the avocado mix onto the toasted bread.

5. Sprinkle feta cheese and pomegranate seeds over the top, then add a pinch of chili flakes for a kick.

6. Admire your work for a moment, then dig in.

Nutritional Value (Per Serving):

- Calories: 250
- Protein: 5g
- Carbohydrates: 22g
- Fat: 17g (healthy fats, folks!)
- Fiber: 7g

Recipe 62: Zesty Quinoa Salad

Preparation Time: 20 minutes

Cooking Time: 40 minutes

Total Time: 1 hour

Category: Side Dish

Quinoa—once the humble grain of the Andes, now the superstar of every health enthusiast's pantry. But this isn't just any quinoa salad; this one's got sass. Imagine it as the dish you bring to a potluck that has everyone asking for the recipe. It's light, it's refreshing, and it's got a zing that'll have you coming back for seconds.

Ingredients:

- 1 cup quinoa
- 2 cups water or vegetable broth
- 1/2 cup cherry tomatoes, halved
- 1/2 cucumber, diced
- 1/4 cup red onion, finely chopped
- 1/4 cup feta cheese, crumbled
- 1/4 cup fresh parsley, chopped
- 2 tbsp olive oil
- 1 tbsp lemon juice
- 1 tsp Dijon mustard
- Salt and pepper to taste

Materials:

- Saucepan with lid
- Large mixing bowl
- Whisk
- Knife and cutting board

Procedure:

1. Rinse the quinoa under cold water (seriously, don't skip this step unless you like bitter quinoa).
2. In a saucepan, bring water or vegetable broth to a boil, then add the quinoa. Reduce the heat, cover, and let it simmer for about 15 minutes, or until all the liquid is absorbed.
3. Fluff the cooked quinoa with a fork and set it aside to cool.
4. In a large mixing bowl, combine the cherry tomatoes, cucumber, red onion, feta, and parsley.
5. In a small bowl, whisk together the olive oil, lemon juice, Dijon mustard, salt, and pepper.
6. Pour the dressing over the salad and toss to combine.
7. Serve chilled or at room temperature—it's all good.

Nutritional Value (Per Serving):

- Calories: 220
- Protein: 6g
- Carbohydrates: 28g
- Fat: 10g
- Fiber: 4g

Recipe 63: Spicy Cauliflower Buffalo Wings

Preparation Time: 10 minutes

Cooking Time: 30 minutes

Total Time: 40 minutes

Category: Appetizer

Buffalo wings are great, but they're not exactly on speaking terms with your waistline. Enter cauliflower—your new best friend. These spicy little bites will have you questioning why you ever bothered with the chicken version. Perfect for game day, or, you know, any day you want a kick in your snack routine.

Ingredients:

- 1 head of cauliflower, cut into florets
- 1/2 cup all-purpose flour (or gluten-free flour)
- 1/2 cup water
- 1/2 tsp garlic powder
- 1/2 tsp paprika
- 1/2 tsp salt
- 1/4 tsp black pepper
- 1/2 cup hot sauce (like Frank's RedHot)
- 2 tbsp butter, melted

Materials:

- Baking sheet
- Parchment paper
- Large mixing bowl
- Small saucepan

Procedure:

1. Preheat your oven to 425°F (220°C) and line a baking sheet with parchment paper.
2. In a large mixing bowl, whisk together the flour, water, garlic powder, paprika, salt, and pepper until smooth.
3. Add the cauliflower florets to the batter, making sure they're well-coated.
4. Spread the coated cauliflower on the baking sheet in a single layer.

5. Bake for 20-25 minutes, flipping halfway through, until they're golden and crispy.

6. While the cauliflower bakes, heat the hot sauce and melted butter in a small saucepan over medium heat, stirring until combined.

7. Remove the cauliflower from the oven and toss it in the hot sauce mixture.

8. Return the cauliflower to the oven for another 5-10 minutes until they're sizzling.

9. Serve with a side of celery sticks and some ranch or blue cheese dip if you're feeling fancy.

Nutritional Value (Per Serving):

- Calories: 150
- Protein: 3g
- Carbohydrates: 15g
- Fat: 9g
- Fiber: 4g

Recipe 64: Creamy Avocado Pasta

Preparation Time: 10 minutes

Cooking Time: 10 minutes

Total Time: 20 minutes

Category: Entrée

When you're craving something creamy but don't want to commit carbicide, this avocado pasta is your go-to. It's rich, it's velvety, and it's green—so you can tell yourself it's basically a salad. Perfect for a quick weeknight dinner that'll make you feel like you've mastered the art of Italian cuisine.

Ingredients:

- 8 oz whole wheat pasta
- 1 ripe avocado
- 1 clove garlic, minced
- 1/4 cup fresh basil leaves
- 2 tbsp lemon juice
- 1/4 cup extra-virgin olive oil
- Salt and pepper to taste
- Cherry tomatoes for garnish (optional)

Materials:

- Large pot
- Blender or food processor
- Mixing bowl

Procedure:

1. Cook the pasta according to package instructions until al dente. Drain and set aside.
2. In a blender or food processor, combine the avocado, garlic, basil, lemon juice, olive oil, salt, and pepper. Blend until smooth.
3. Toss the cooked pasta with the avocado sauce until evenly coated.
4. Garnish with cherry tomatoes if desired, and serve immediately.

Nutritional Value (Per Serving):

- Calories: 380
- Protein: 9g
- Carbohydrates: 40g
- Fat: 20g
- Fiber: 8g

Recipe 65: Berry Bliss Smoothie Bowl

Preparation Time: 10 minutes

Cooking Time: 10 minutes

Total Time: 20 minutes

Category: Dessert

Here's a dessert that's basically breakfast in disguise. It's like having a bowl of ice cream, but this time, you can pat yourself on the back for making a healthy choice. Each spoonful is packed with antioxidants and a burst of berry goodness that'll make you feel like you're indulging in something way naughtier.

Ingredients:

- 1 banana, frozen
- 1/2 cup mixed berries (blueberries, strawberries, raspberries)
- 1/4 cup Greek yogurt
- 1/4 cup almond milk
- 1 tbsp honey
- 1 tbsp chia seeds
- Granola, fresh berries, and coconut flakes for topping

Materials:

- Blender
- Bowl
- Spoon

Procedure:

1. Add the frozen banana, mixed berries, Greek yogurt, almond milk, and honey to a blender. Blend until smooth and creamy.
2. Pour the smoothie into a bowl.
3. Top with granola, fresh berries, coconut flakes, and a sprinkle of chia seeds.
4. Grab a spoon and dive into this guilt-free treat.

Nutritional Value (Per Serving):

- Calories: 250
- Protein: 8g
- Carbohydrates: 45g
- Fat: 6g
- Fiber: 8g

Recipe 66: Ginger-Turmeric Detox Soup

Preparation Time: 15 minutes

Cooking Time: 30 minutes

Total Time: 45 minutes

Category: Entrée

After a weekend of indulgence, your body's crying out for a reset. Enter this detox soup—a golden elixir that'll have you feeling virtuous with every sip.

It's like a spa day in a bowl, with the warm kick of ginger and the earthy richness of turmeric guiding you back to wellness.

Ingredients:

- 1 tbsp olive oil
- 1 onion, chopped
- 2 cloves garlic, minced
- 1-inch piece ginger, grated
- 1 tsp turmeric powder
- 4 cups vegetable broth
- 2 carrots, sliced
- 1 sweet potato, diced
- 1 can coconut milk
- Salt and pepper to taste
- Fresh cilantro for garnish

Materials:

- Large pot
- Wooden spoon

Procedure:

1. Heat the olive oil in a large pot over medium heat. Add the chopped onion and cook until it turns translucent.
2. Stir in the garlic and ginger, cooking until fragrant—just about a minute or so.
3. Add the turmeric powder and stir to combine, letting it cook for another minute to release its flavor.

4. Pour in the vegetable broth, followed by the carrots and sweet potato. Bring the soup to a boil, then reduce the heat and let it simmer for 20-25 minutes, or until the vegetables are tender.

5. Stir in the coconut milk, and season with salt and pepper. Let the soup simmer for another 5 minutes.

6. Ladle the soup into bowls, garnish with fresh cilantro, and enjoy the warmth and comfort of this healing dish.

Nutritional Value (Per Serving):

- Calories: 280
- Protein: 5g
- Carbohydrates: 30g
- Fat: 16g
- Fiber: 6g

Recipe 67: Crispy Baked Sweet Potato Fries

Preparation Time: 15 minutes

Cooking Time: 30 minutes

Total Time: 45 minutes

Category: Side Dish

Who said fries have to be deep-fried and drenched in guilt? These crispy baked sweet potato fries are here to prove that healthy can be delicious.

Perfect for when you're craving something salty and satisfying, with a hint of sweetness to keep things interesting.

Ingredients:

- 2 large sweet potatoes
- 2 tbsp olive oil
- 1 tsp paprika
- 1/2 tsp garlic powder
- Salt and pepper to taste
- Fresh parsley for garnish

Materials:

- Baking sheet
- Parchment paper
- Large mixing bowl
- Knife and cutting board

Procedure:

1. Preheat your oven to 425°F (220°C) and line a baking sheet with parchment paper.
2. Peel the sweet potatoes and cut them into thin fries—aim for even sizes so they cook uniformly.
3. Toss the sweet potato fries in a large bowl with olive oil, paprika, garlic powder, salt, and pepper.
4. Spread the fries in a single layer on the baking sheet, making sure they're not touching (they need space to crisp up!).

5. Bake for 25-30 minutes, flipping halfway through, until they're golden and crispy.

6. Sprinkle with fresh parsley and serve hot. Dip them in your favorite sauce or enjoy them as is.

Nutritional Value (Per Serving):

- Calories: 180
- Protein: 2g
- Carbohydrates: 32g
- Fat: 7g
- Fiber: 5g

Recipe 68: Stuffed Bell Peppers

Preparation Time: 20 minutes
Cooking Time: 30-35 minutes
Total Time: 50-55 minutes
Category: Entrée

Stuffed bell peppers are like a little gift to yourself—each one filled with savory goodness that's both satisfying and nutritious. Imagine biting into a tender pepper, the juices mixing with a rich filling that's bursting with flavor. This is comfort food at its finest, with a healthy twist.

Ingredients:

- 4 large bell peppers (any color)
- 1 cup quinoa, cooked

- 1/2 lb ground turkey or chicken
- 1/2 onion, diced
- 2 cloves garlic, minced
- 1 tsp cumin
- 1 tsp paprika
- 1 can diced tomatoes, drained
- 1/2 cup shredded mozzarella cheese
- Salt and pepper to taste
- Fresh cilantro for garnish

Materials:

- Large skillet
- Baking dish
- Aluminum foil
- Knife and cutting board

Procedure:

1. Preheat your oven to 375°F (190°C). Cut the tops off the bell peppers and remove the seeds and membranes. Set aside.

2. In a large skillet, cook the ground turkey or chicken over medium heat until browned. Add the diced onion and garlic, cooking until softened.

3. Stir in the cooked quinoa, cumin, paprika, and diced tomatoes. Season with salt and pepper to taste. Let the mixture cook for a few minutes to combine the flavors.

4. Stuff each bell pepper with the quinoa mixture and place them in a baking dish.

5. Cover the dish with aluminum foil and bake for 25 minutes.

6. Remove the foil, sprinkle the tops of the peppers with shredded mozzarella, and bake for another 10 minutes, or until the cheese is melted and bubbly.

7. Garnish with fresh cilantro and serve hot.

Nutritional Value (Per Serving):

- Calories: 320
- Protein: 25g
- Carbohydrates: 30g
- Fat: 10g
- Fiber: 7g

Recipe 69: Lemon-Garlic Roasted Brussels Sprouts

Preparation Time: 10 minutes

Cooking Time: 25 minutes

Total Time: 35 minutes

Category: Side Dish

Brussels sprouts get a bad rap, but let me tell you, when they're roasted to crispy perfection and infused with lemon and garlic, they're downright addictive. This is the kind of side dish that might just steal the spotlight from the main course. Don't be surprised if you find yourself munching on them straight from the pan.

Ingredients:

- 1 lb Brussels sprouts, trimmed and halved
- 2 tbsp olive oil
- 2 cloves garlic, minced
- Zest and juice of 1 lemon
- Salt and pepper to taste
- Parmesan cheese for garnish (optional)

Materials:

- Baking sheet
- Parchment paper
- Mixing bowl

Procedure:

1. Preheat your oven to 400°F (200°C) and line a baking sheet with parchment paper.

2. Toss the Brussels sprouts in a mixing bowl with olive oil, minced garlic, lemon zest, salt, and pepper.

3. Spread the Brussels sprouts in a single layer on the baking sheet, cut side down for maximum caramelization.

4. Roast for 20-25 minutes, until they're golden and crispy on the edges.

5. Remove from the oven, and drizzle with lemon juice.

6. If you're feeling indulgent, sprinkle some Parmesan cheese over the top before serving.

Nutritional Value (Per Serving):

- Calories: 110
- Protein: 4g
- Carbohydrates: 12g
- Fat: 7g
- Fiber: 4g

Recipe 70: Mango-Chia Pudding

Preparation Time: 10 minutes

Cooking Time: None

Marinating Time: 4 hours (or overnight)

Total Time: 4 hours 10 minutes (or overnight)

Category: Dessert

Chia pudding is like dessert and breakfast had a love child. And when you add mango to the mix? Oh, it's tropical bliss in every bite. This is the kind of dessert that makes you feel like you're on a beach, even if you're just chilling on your couch. It's creamy, sweet, and good for you—what's not to love?

Ingredients:

- 1 cup almond milk
- 3 tbsp chia seeds
- 1 tbsp maple syrup
- 1 ripe mango, diced
- 1/2 tsp vanilla extract
- Fresh mint for garnish (optional)

Materials:

- Mason jar or small bowls
- Mixing spoon

Procedure:

1. In a mason jar or small bowl, combine the almond milk, chia seeds, maple syrup, and vanilla extract. Stir well to combine.
2. Let the mixture sit for 5 minutes, then stir again to prevent clumping.
3. Cover and refrigerate for at least 2 hours, or overnight for a thicker consistency.
4. When ready to serve, top the chia pudding with diced mango and a sprig of fresh mint.
5. Enjoy this creamy, tropical treat that's perfect any time of day.

Nutritional Value (Per Serving):

- Calories: 180

- Protein: 4g

- Carbohydrates: 28g

- Fat: 7g

- Fiber: 10g

Recipe 71: Greek Yogurt Parfait with Mixed Berries

Preparation Time: 5 minutes

Cooking Time: None

Marinating Time: None

Total Time: 5 minutes

Category: Breakfast/Dessert

Parfaits are like the ultimate breakfast hack—they look fancy, taste incredible, and are ridiculously easy to put together. Plus, when you layer in creamy Greek yogurt with a handful of berries, you've got a dessert-worthy treat that's actually good for you.

Ingredients:

- 1 cup Greek yogurt
- 1/2 cup mixed berries (blueberries, strawberries, raspberries)
- 2 tbsp granola
- 1 tbsp honey or maple syrup
- Fresh mint for garnish

Materials:

- Mason jar or tall glass
- Spoon

Procedure:

1. In a mason jar or glass, layer 1/3 cup of Greek yogurt at the bottom.
2. Add a layer of mixed berries, followed by a drizzle of honey or maple syrup.
3. Sprinkle a tablespoon of granola on top.
4. Repeat the layers until you reach the top of the jar.
5. Garnish with a sprig of fresh mint and enjoy immediately.

Nutritional Value (Per Serving):

- Calories: 220
- Protein: 10g
- Carbohydrates: 28g
- Fat: 8g
- Fiber: 4g

Recipe 72: Quinoa & Black Bean Salad

Preparation Time: 15 minutes

Cooking Time: 20 minutes

Marinating Time: None

Total Time: 35 minutes

Category: Side Dish/Entrée

This salad is the perfect blend of wholesome ingredients and vibrant flavors. Whether you're packing it for lunch or serving it as a side, it's sure to impress. And the best part? It keeps you full and energized without weighing you down.

Ingredients:

- 1 cup cooked quinoa
- 1 can black beans, rinsed and drained
- 1 red bell pepper, diced
- 1/2 red onion, finely chopped
- 1/2 cup corn kernels (fresh or frozen)

- 1 avocado, diced
- 1/4 cup fresh cilantro, chopped
- Juice of 1 lime
- 2 tbsp olive oil
- Salt and pepper to taste

Materials:

- Large mixing bowl
- Knife and cutting board
- Serving spoon

Procedure:

1. In a large mixing bowl, combine the cooked quinoa, black beans, red bell pepper, red onion, and corn.
2. Drizzle with lime juice and olive oil, then toss to combine.
3. Gently fold in the diced avocado and fresh cilantro.
4. Season with salt and pepper to taste, and serve chilled or at room temperature.

Nutritional Value (Per Serving):

- Calories: 310
- Protein: 10g
- Carbohydrates: 45g
- Fat: 12g
- Fiber: 10g

Recipe 73: Garlic & Herb Grilled Chicken

Preparation Time: 10 minutes

Cooking Time: 15-20 minutes

Marinating Time: 30 minutes (optional)

Total Time: 55-60 minutes (including marinating time)

Category: Entrée

Grilled chicken doesn't have to be boring! This recipe is all about infusing juicy chicken breasts with the flavors of garlic, fresh herbs, and a hint of lemon. It's quick to prepare and perfect for any meal, from a casual family dinner to a summer BBQ.

Ingredients:

- 4 boneless, skinless chicken breasts
- 3 cloves garlic, minced
- 2 tbsp olive oil
- Juice of 1 lemon
- 2 tbsp fresh parsley, chopped
- 1 tbsp fresh thyme leaves
- Salt and pepper to taste

Materials:

- Grill or grill pan
- Mixing bowl
- Tongs

Procedure:

1. In a mixing bowl, combine the minced garlic, olive oil, lemon juice, parsley, thyme, salt, and pepper.
2. Add the chicken breasts, making sure each one is well coated with the marinade. Let it sit for at least 30 minutes, or up to 4 hours in the refrigerator.
3. Preheat the grill or grill pan over medium-high heat.
4. Grill the chicken for 6-7 minutes per side, or until fully cooked and no longer pink inside.
5. Serve hot with your favorite sides.

Nutritional Value (Per Serving):

- Calories: 220
- Protein: 25g
- Carbohydrates: 2g
- Fat: 12g
- Fiber: 1g

Recipe 74: Spaghetti Squash with Tomato Basil Sauce

Preparation Time: 10 minutes

Cooking Time: 40-45 minutes

Marinating Time: None

Total Time: 50-55 minutes

Category: Entrée

If you're looking for a low-carb alternative to pasta, spaghetti squash is your new best friend. This dish is all about keeping things light and flavorful, with a simple tomato basil sauce that lets the squash shine.

Ingredients:

- 1 large spaghetti squash
- 2 tbsp olive oil
- 1 can (15 oz) diced tomatoes
- 3 cloves garlic, minced
- 1/4 cup fresh basil, chopped
- Salt and pepper to taste
- Grated Parmesan cheese for garnish (optional)

Materials:

- Baking sheet
- Large skillet
- Fork
- Knife and cutting board

Procedure:

1. Preheat your oven to 400°F (200°C). Cut the spaghetti squash in half lengthwise, and scoop out the seeds.

2. Drizzle the squash halves with 1 tablespoon of olive oil and season with salt and pepper. Place them cut side down on a baking sheet and roast for 35-40 minutes, or until tender.

3. While the squash is roasting, heat the remaining tablespoon of olive oil in a skillet over medium heat. Add the minced garlic and cook until fragrant.

4. Stir in the diced tomatoes and fresh basil, and let the sauce simmer for 10-15 minutes. Season with salt and pepper.

5. Once the squash is done, use a fork to scrape out the flesh, which will come apart in spaghetti-like strands.

6. Top the spaghetti squash with the tomato basil sauce, and garnish with grated Parmesan cheese if desired.

Nutritional Value (Per Serving):

- Calories: 170
- Protein: 4g
- Carbohydrates: 30g
- Fat: 6g
- Fiber: 8g

Recipe 75: Avocado Toast with Poached Eggs

Preparation Time: 10 minutes

Cooking Time: 5 minutes

Marinating Time: None

Total Time: 15 minutes

Category: Breakfast/Brunch

Avocado toast is a classic, but when you add a perfectly poached egg on top? That's when it becomes next-level. This is the kind of breakfast that feels indulgent yet is packed with good-for-you ingredients. Plus, it's Instagram-worthy—if you're into that sort of thing.

Ingredients:

- 2 slices whole-grain bread, toasted
- 1 ripe avocado
- 2 eggs
- 1 tbsp vinegar
- 1/2 tsp red pepper flakes
- Salt and pepper to taste
- Fresh herbs for garnish (optional)

Materials:

- Toaster
- Small saucepan
- Slotted spoon
- Knife and cutting board

Procedure:

1. Bring a small saucepan of water to a gentle simmer. Add the vinegar.
2. Crack each egg into a small bowl, then gently slide it into the simmering water. Poach the eggs for 3-4 minutes, or until the whites are set and the yolks are still runny.

3. While the eggs are poaching, mash the avocado with a fork and season with salt, pepper, and red pepper flakes.

4. Spread the mashed avocado onto the toasted bread.

5. Carefully remove the poached eggs with a slotted spoon and place one on each slice of toast.

6. Garnish with fresh herbs if desired, and serve immediately.

Nutritional Value (Per Serving):

- Calories: 320
- Protein: 14g
- Carbohydrates: 28g
- Fat: 20g
- Fiber: 8g

Recipe 76: Zucchini Noodles with Pesto

Preparation Time: 10 minutes

Cooking Time: 5 minutes

Total Time: 15 minutes

Category: Entrée

Zucchini noodles, or "zoodles," are the ultimate way to satisfy your pasta cravings without the carb overload. Toss them in a fresh, vibrant pesto sauce, and you've got a dish that's as refreshing as it is satisfying.

Ingredients:

- 4 medium zucchini, spiralized
- 1/2 cup fresh basil leaves
- 1/4 cup pine nuts
- 1/4 cup Parmesan cheese, grated
- 2 cloves garlic, minced
- 1/4 cup olive oil
- Salt and pepper to taste
- Cherry tomatoes for garnish (optional)

Materials:

- Spiralizer
- Blender or food processor
- Large skillet

Procedure:

1. Spiralize the zucchini into noodles using a spiralizer and set aside.
2. In a blender or food processor, combine the basil leaves, pine nuts, Parmesan cheese, and garlic. Pulse until finely chopped.
3. With the blender running, slowly pour in the olive oil until the pesto is smooth. Season with salt and pepper to taste.
4. Heat a large skillet over medium heat. Add the zucchini noodles and cook for 2-3 minutes, just until they start to soften.
5. Remove the skillet from the heat and toss the zoodles with the pesto sauce.
6. Garnish with cherry tomatoes and serve immediately.

Nutritional Value (Per Serving):

- Calories: 180
- Protein: 6g
- Carbohydrates: 10g
- Fat: 14g
- Fiber: 4g

Recipe 77: Berry Almond Smoothie

Preparation Time: 5 minutes

Cooking Time: None

Marinating Time: None

Total Time: 5 minutes

Category: Breakfast/Snack

Smoothies are the busy person's best friend. They're quick, customizable, and can be packed with all sorts of nutritious goodies. This Berry Almond Smoothie is a refreshing, protein-rich option that'll kickstart your day or give you a perfect midday boost.

Ingredients:

- 1 cup mixed berries (strawberries, blueberries, raspberries)
- 1/2 banana
- 1/2 cup almond milk
- 1/4 cup Greek yogurt
- 1 tbsp almond butter
- 1 tbsp honey or maple syrup (optional)
- 1/2 tsp vanilla extract
- 1 tbsp chia seeds (optional)

Materials:

- Blender
- Glass

Procedure:

1. Add all the ingredients to a blender.

2. Blend on high until smooth and creamy.

3. Taste and adjust sweetness with honey or maple syrup if desired.

4. Pour into a glass and enjoy immediately.

Nutritional Value (Per Serving):

- Calories: 250
- Protein: 10g
- Carbohydrates: 35g
- Fat: 9g
- Fiber: 8g

Recipe 78: Sweet Potato and Black Bean Tacos

Preparation Time: 15 minutes

Cooking Time: 25 minutes

Marinating Time: None

Total Time: 40 minutes

Category: Entrée

Who says tacos can't be healthy? These Sweet Potato and Black Bean Tacos are hearty, flavorful, and loaded with all the good stuff. They're also a fantastic meatless option that even carnivores will love.

Ingredients:

- 2 large sweet potatoes, peeled and diced
- 1 tbsp olive oil
- 1 tsp cumin

- 1/2 tsp smoked paprika
- Salt and pepper to taste
- 1 can black beans, rinsed and drained
- 8 small corn tortillas
- 1/2 cup avocado, sliced
- 1/4 cup fresh cilantro, chopped
- 1/4 cup salsa or pico de gallo
- Lime wedges for serving

Materials:

- Baking sheet
- Mixing bowl
- Skillet

Procedure:

1. Preheat the oven to 400°F (200°C).
2. In a mixing bowl, toss the diced sweet potatoes with olive oil, cumin, smoked paprika, salt, and pepper.
3. Spread the sweet potatoes on a baking sheet and roast for 25-30 minutes, or until tender and slightly crispy on the edges.
4. While the sweet potatoes are roasting, warm the tortillas in a skillet over medium heat.
5. Assemble the tacos by filling each tortilla with roasted sweet potatoes, black beans, avocado slices, cilantro, and a spoonful of salsa.
6. Serve with lime wedges and enjoy.

Nutritional Value (Per Serving):

- Calories: 180
- Protein: 5g
- Carbohydrates: 35g
- Fat: 5g
- Fiber: 8g

Recipe 79: Lemon Garlic Shrimp Skewers

Preparation Time: 10 minutes

Cooking Time: 5-7 minutes

Marinating Time: 15-30 minutes (optional)

Total Time: 30-45 minutes (including marinating time)

Category: Appetizer/Entrée

These shrimp skewers are the perfect blend of zesty and savory, making them an excellent choice for grilling season. They're quick to prepare and impressive enough to serve at your next gathering—just be prepared for everyone to ask for the recipe!

Ingredients:

- 1 lb large shrimp, peeled and deveined
- 2 tbsp olive oil
- 3 cloves garlic, minced
- Juice of 1 lemon
- 1 tsp lemon zest
- 1 tbsp fresh parsley, chopped
- Salt and pepper to taste
- Wooden or metal skewers

Materials:

- Skewers
- Grill or grill pan
- Mixing bowl

Procedure:

1. In a mixing bowl, combine olive oil, minced garlic, lemon juice, lemon zest, parsley, salt, and pepper.
2. Add the shrimp to the bowl and toss to coat evenly. Let it marinate for 15-20 minutes.
3. Preheat the grill or grill pan to medium-high heat.
4. Thread the shrimp onto skewers, making sure they're not too tightly packed.
5. Grill the shrimp for 2-3 minutes per side, or until they're pink and opaque.
6. Serve hot, garnished with extra parsley and lemon wedges if desired.

Nutritional Value (Per Serving):

- Calories: 150
- Protein: 24g
- Carbohydrates: 2g
- Fat: 5g
- Fiber: 0g

Recipe 80: Chocolate Chia Pudding

Preparation Time: 5 minutes

Cooking Time: None

Marinating Time: 4 hours (or overnight)

Total Time: 4 hours 5 minutes (or overnight)

Category: Dessert/Breakfast

This pudding is like having dessert for breakfast—except it's packed with omega-3s, fiber, and protein. The best part? It takes just minutes to prepare and can be made the night before.

Ingredients:

- 1/4 cup chia seeds
- 1 cup almond milk
- 2 tbsp cocoa powder
- 1-2 tbsp maple syrup or honey
- 1/2 tsp vanilla extract
- Fresh berries or shaved chocolate for topping

Materials:

- Mixing bowl
- Whisk
- Serving bowls or jars

Procedure:

1. In a mixing bowl, whisk together the chia seeds, almond milk, cocoa powder, maple syrup, and vanilla extract.
2. Cover and refrigerate for at least 4 hours, or overnight, until the pudding is thickened.
3. Give the pudding a good stir and divide it into serving bowls or jars.
4. Top with fresh berries or shaved chocolate and serve.

Nutritional Value (Per Serving):

- Calories: 180
- Protein: 5g
- Carbohydrates: 20g
- Fat: 9g

- Fiber: 10g

Recipe 81: Roasted Brussels Sprouts with Balsamic Glaze

Preparation Time: 10 minutes

Cooking Time: 25 minutes

Marinating Time: None

Total Time: 35 minutes

Category: Side Dish

Brussels sprouts have had a major glow-up in recent years, and this recipe shows why. Roasting them brings out a delicious caramelized flavor, and the balsamic glaze adds just the right amount of tangy sweetness.

Ingredients:

- 1 lb Brussels sprouts, trimmed and halved
- 2 tbsp olive oil
- Salt and pepper to taste
- 2 tbsp balsamic vinegar
- 1 tbsp honey

Materials:

- Baking sheet
- Small saucepan
- Mixing bowl

Procedure:

1. Preheat the oven to 425°F (220°C).
2. Toss the Brussels sprouts in olive oil, salt, and pepper, and spread them on a baking sheet.
3. Roast for 20-25 minutes, shaking the pan halfway through, until the sprouts are crispy on the outside and tender on the inside.
4. While the sprouts are roasting, heat the balsamic vinegar and honey in a small saucepan over medium heat, stirring until the mixture thickens slightly.
5. Drizzle the balsamic glaze over the roasted Brussels sprouts and serve immediately.

Nutritional Value (Per Serving):

- Calories: 150
- Protein: 4g
- Carbohydrates: 18g
- Fat: 7g
- Fiber: 6g

Recipe 82: Spinach & Feta Stuffed Chicken Breasts

Preparation Time: 15 minutes

Cooking Time: 25-30 minutes

Marinating Time: None

Total Time: 40-45 minutes

Category: Entrée

If you want to impress your dinner guests (or just treat yourself), these stuffed chicken breasts are the way to go. The combination of spinach and feta makes for a flavorful, slightly tangy filling that turns simple chicken breasts into a gourmet dish.

Ingredients:

- 4 boneless, skinless chicken breasts
- 1 cup fresh spinach, chopped
- 1/2 cup feta cheese, crumbled
- 2 cloves garlic, minced
- 1 tbsp olive oil
- Salt and pepper to taste
- Toothpicks or kitchen twine

Materials:

- Skillet
- Oven-safe dish
- Knife and cutting board

Procedure:

1. Preheat the oven to 375°F (190°C).
2. In a small bowl, mix together the chopped spinach, feta cheese, and minced garlic.

3. Cut a pocket into each chicken breast, being careful not to cut all the way through.

4. Stuff the spinach and feta mixture into each pocket and secure with toothpicks or kitchen twine.

5. Heat the olive oil in a skillet over medium heat. Sear the chicken breasts for 2-3 minutes on each side until browned.

6. Transfer the chicken to an oven-safe dish and bake for 20-25 minutes, or until fully cooked.

7. Serve hot, with your favorite sides.

Nutritional Value (Per Serving):

- Calories: 280
- Protein: 35g
- Carbohydrates: 3g
- Fat: 14g
- Fiber: 1g

Recipe 83: Cauliflower Rice Stir-Fry

Preparation Time: 10 minutes

Cooking Time: 15 minutes

Marinating Time: None

Total Time: 25 minutes

Category: Side Dish/Entrée

Cauliflower rice is a genius low-carb alternative to traditional rice, and when it's stir-fried with colorful veggies and a savory sauce, it becomes a dish that even rice lovers will crave.

Ingredients:

- 1 head cauliflower, grated or pulsed in a food processor to resemble rice
- 1 red bell pepper, diced
- 1 carrot, julienned
- 1/2 cup frozen peas
- 2 cloves garlic, minced
- 2 tbsp soy sauce or tamari
- 1 tbsp sesame oil
- 2 green onions, sliced
- 1 tbsp sesame seeds for garnish (optional)

Materials:

- Food processor (optional)
- Large skillet or wok

Procedure:

1. Heat the sesame oil in a large skillet or wok over medium heat.
2. Add the minced garlic and sauté for 1 minute until fragrant.
3. Add the bell pepper, carrot, and peas, and stir-fry for 3-4 minutes until the vegetables are tender.
4. Add the cauliflower rice and soy sauce. Stir-fry for another 5 minutes, or until the cauliflower is tender.
5. Stir in the green onions and cook for another 1-2 minutes.
6. Serve hot, garnished with sesame seeds if desired.

Nutritional Value (Per Serving):

- Calories: 120
- Protein: 4g
- Carbohydrates: 16g
- Fat: 5g
- Fiber: 5g

Recipe 84: Zucchini Noodles with Pesto

Preparation Time: 10 minutes

Cooking Time: 5 minutes

Marinating Time: None

Total Time: 15 minutes

Category: Entrée/Side Dish

Zucchini noodles, or "zoodles," are a fantastic pasta alternative for those looking to cut carbs without sacrificing flavor. Paired with a fresh basil pesto, this dish is light, vibrant, and packed with nutrients.

Ingredients:

- 2 large zucchinis, spiralized into noodles
- 1/2 cup fresh basil leaves
- 1/4 cup pine nuts or walnuts
- 1/4 cup Parmesan cheese, grated
- 1 clove garlic
- 1/4 cup olive oil
- Salt and pepper to taste
- Cherry tomatoes for garnish (optional)

Materials:

- Spiralizer
- Food processor
- Skillet

Procedure:

1. In a food processor, combine basil leaves, pine nuts, Parmesan cheese, and garlic. Pulse until finely chopped.
2. With the processor running, slowly add olive oil until the pesto is smooth and creamy. Season with salt and pepper.
3. Heat a skillet over medium heat and lightly sauté the zucchini noodles for 2-3 minutes, just until tender.
4. Toss the warm zucchini noodles with the pesto sauce until evenly coated.
5. Garnish with cherry tomatoes if desired, and serve immediately.

Nutritional Value (Per Serving):

- Calories: 200
- Protein: 6g
- Carbohydrates: 8g
- Fat: 18g
- Fiber: 3g

Recipe 85: Pumpkin Soup

Preparation Time: 10 minutes

Cooking Time: 30 minutes

Marinating Time: None

Total Time: 40 minutes

Category: Soup/Entrée

There's nothing quite as comforting as a warm bowl of pumpkin soup on a chilly day. This creamy and slightly sweet soup is perfect as a starter or a light main course, especially when served with crusty bread.

Ingredients:

- 1 can (15 oz) pumpkin puree
- 1 onion, diced
- 2 cloves garlic, minced
- 1 tbsp olive oil
- 2 cups vegetable broth
- 1 cup coconut milk
- 1 tsp ground cinnamon
- 1/2 tsp ground nutmeg
- Salt and pepper to taste
- Pumpkin seeds for garnish (optional)

Materials:

- Large pot
- Blender or immersion blender

Procedure:

1. In a large pot, heat the olive oil over medium heat. Add the diced onion and garlic, and sauté until softened, about 5 minutes.
2. Stir in the pumpkin puree, vegetable broth, cinnamon, and nutmeg. Bring the mixture to a simmer.
3. Reduce heat and simmer for 10 minutes, stirring occasionally.
4. Use a blender or immersion blender to puree the soup until smooth.
5. Stir in the coconut milk and season with salt and pepper.
6. Serve hot, garnished with pumpkin seeds if desired.

Nutritional Value (Per Serving):

- Calories: 150
- Protein: 3g
- Carbohydrates: 18g
- Fat: 7g
- Fiber: 4g

Recipe 86: Quinoa Salad with Lemon Vinaigrette

Preparation Time: 15 minutes

Cooking Time: 20 minutes

Marinating Time: None

Total Time: 35 minutes

Category: Salad/Side Dish

Quinoa is often hailed as a superfood, and for good reason. This grain is packed with protein, fiber, and essential nutrients. This salad, tossed with fresh vegetables and a tangy lemon vinaigrette, is both refreshing and filling.

Ingredients:

- 1 cup quinoa, rinsed
- 2 cups water
- 1 cucumber, diced
- 1 red bell pepper, diced
- 1/4 cup red onion, finely chopped
- 1/4 cup fresh parsley, chopped
- 1/4 cup crumbled feta cheese (optional)
- Juice of 1 lemon
- 1/4 cup olive oil
- Salt and pepper to taste

Materials:

- Medium pot
- Mixing bowl

Procedure:

1. In a medium pot, combine the quinoa and water. Bring to a boil, then reduce heat to low and cover. Simmer for 15 minutes, or until the water is absorbed and the quinoa is fluffy. Let it cool.

2. In a large mixing bowl, combine the cooled quinoa, cucumber, bell pepper, red onion, parsley, and feta cheese if using.

3. In a small bowl, whisk together the lemon juice, olive oil, salt, and pepper.

4. Pour the vinaigrette over the salad and toss to coat evenly.

5. Serve chilled or at room temperature.

Nutritional Value (Per Serving):

- Calories: 200
- Protein: 6g
- Carbohydrates: 24g
- Fat: 10g
- Fiber: 4g

Recipe 87: Baked Salmon with Garlic and Dill

Preparation Time: 10 minutes

Cooking Time: 15-20 minutes

Marinating Time: None

Total Time: 25-30 minutes

Category: Entrée

Salmon is a powerhouse of omega-3s and is incredibly versatile. This baked version, with a simple garlic and dill seasoning, lets the fish's natural flavors shine. It's perfect for a quick weeknight dinner.

Ingredients:

- 4 salmon fillets
- 2 tbsp olive oil
- 2 cloves garlic, minced
- 1 tbsp fresh dill, chopped
- Juice of 1/2 lemon
- Salt and pepper to taste
- Lemon wedges for serving

Materials:

- Baking sheet
- Aluminum foil

Procedure:

1. Preheat the oven to 375°F (190°C).
2. Place the salmon fillets on a baking sheet lined with aluminum foil.
3. In a small bowl, mix together olive oil, garlic, dill, lemon juice, salt, and pepper.
4. Brush the mixture over the salmon fillets.
5. Fold the foil over the salmon to create a sealed packet.
6. Bake for 15-20 minutes, or until the salmon is cooked through and flakes easily with a fork.
7. Serve with lemon wedges on the side.

Nutritional Value (Per Serving):

- Calories: 250

- Protein: 25g

- Carbohydrates: 1g

- Fat: 15g

- Fiber: 0g

Recipe 88: Stuffed Bell Peppers

Preparation Time: 20 minutes

Cooking Time: 30-35 minutes

Marinating Time: None

Total Time: 50-55 minutes

Category: Entrée

Stuffed bell peppers are a classic dish that can be customized in countless ways. This version is filled with a savory mix of ground turkey, rice, and vegetables, making it a hearty and satisfying meal.

Ingredients:

- 4 large bell peppers, tops cut off and seeds removed
- 1 lb ground turkey or beef
- 1 cup cooked rice (white or brown)
- 1 onion, diced
- 2 cloves garlic, minced
- 1 can (14.5 oz) diced tomatoes, drained
- 1 tsp Italian seasoning
- Salt and pepper to taste
- 1/2 cup shredded cheese (optional)

Materials:

- Large skillet
- Baking dish

Procedure:

1. Preheat the oven to 375°F (190°C).
2. In a large skillet, cook the ground turkey or beef over medium heat until browned. Drain any excess fat.

3. Add the diced onion and garlic to the skillet and sauté until softened.
4. Stir in the cooked rice, diced tomatoes, Italian seasoning, salt, and pepper.
5. Spoon the mixture into the hollowed-out bell peppers.
6. Place the stuffed peppers in a baking dish and cover with foil.
7. Bake for 25-30 minutes, until the peppers are tender.
8. If using cheese, uncover the peppers, sprinkle with cheese, and bake for an additional 5 minutes until the cheese is melted.
9. Serve hot.

Nutritional Value (Per Serving):

- Calories: 300
- Protein: 25g
- Carbohydrates: 25g
- Fat: 10g
- Fiber: 5g

Recipe 89: Honey Garlic Shrimp

Preparation Time: 10 minutes

Cooking Time: 10 minutes

Marinating TimPe: None

Total Time: 20 minutes

Category: Entrée

Honey garlic shrimp is a sweet and savory delight that comes together in minutes. Perfect for a quick weeknight meal, this dish pairs beautifully with steamed rice or noodles.

Ingredients:

- 1 lb shrimp, peeled and deveined
- 1/4 cup honey
- 1/4 cup soy sauce
- 3 cloves garlic, minced
- 1 tbsp olive oil
- 1 tsp ginger, minced
- Green onions for garnish (optional)

Materials:

- Large skillet
- Mixing bowl

Procedure:

1. In a mixing bowl, combine honey, soy sauce, garlic, and ginger.
2. Add the shrimp to the bowl and let it marinate for at least 15 minutes.
3. Heat olive oil in a large skillet over medium heat.
4. Add the shrimp to the skillet, discarding the marinade, and cook for 2-3 minutes on each side until the shrimp turns pink and opaque.
5. Serve hot, garnished with green onions if desired.

Nutritional Value (Per Serving):

- Calories: 210
- Protein: 24g
- Carbohydrates: 15g
- Fat: 5g

- Fiber: 0g

Recipe 90: Avocado Toast with Poached Egg

Preparation Time: 10 minutes

Cooking Time: 5 minutes

Marinating Time: None

Total Time: 15 minutes

Category: Breakfast/Brunch

Avocado toast is a trendy favorite, and when you top it with a perfectly poached egg, it becomes a protein-packed meal that's hard to resist. It's a delicious way to start your day.

Ingredients:

- 1 ripe avocado
- 2 slices of whole-grain bread
- 2 eggs
- 1 tsp white vinegar (for poaching)
- Salt and pepper to taste
- Red pepper flakes (optional)
- Lemon juice (optional)

Materials:

- Toaster
- Saucepan
- Slotted spoon

Procedure:

1. Toast the slices of bread to your desired level of crispiness.
2. Mash the avocado in a bowl, seasoning with salt, pepper, and a squeeze of lemon juice if desired.
3. Spread the mashed avocado evenly over the toast.

4. To poach the eggs, bring a saucepan of water to a gentle simmer and add the vinegar.

5. Crack each egg into a small bowl, then gently slide the egg into the simmering water.

6. Poach the eggs for 3-4 minutes, or until the whites are set and the yolks are still runny.

7. Remove the eggs with a slotted spoon, letting them drain briefly on a paper towel.

8. Place a poached egg on top of each avocado toast, sprinkle with red pepper flakes if desired, and serve immediately.

Nutritional Value (Per Serving):

- Calories: 320
- Protein: 12g
- Carbohydrates: 24g
- Fat: 20g
- Fiber: 7g

CONCLUSION

The Legacy of TikTok Cooking: Inspiring the Next Generation of Home Cooks

The Impact of TikTok on Culinary Creativity

TikTok has undeniably revolutionized the way we consume and engage with food content. The rise of TikTok cooking has had a profound impact on culinary creativity, ushering in a new era of accessible and interactive cooking experiences. The platform has provided a space for home cooks, aspiring chefs, and food enthusiasts to showcase their skills, share their passion for food, and inspire others with their unique creations.

One of the key impacts of TikTok on culinary creativity is the democratization of cooking knowledge. In the past, culinary expertise was often confined to traditional cooking shows or cookbooks, which limited the reach and accessibility of culinary inspiration. However, TikTok's short-form video format has broken down these barriers, allowing anyone with a smartphone and a passion for cooking to become a content creator and share their recipes with the world. This democratization has empowered individuals from diverse backgrounds to showcase their culinary skills, cultural heritage, and personal cooking styles, fostering a rich and vibrant food community on TikTok.

Furthermore, TikTok has facilitated the rapid spread of culinary trends and innovative cooking techniques. With its algorithmic recommendation system and viral nature, TikTok has become a breeding ground for food trends that capture the attention of millions of users worldwide. From whipped coffee to cloud bread, TikTok's influence on food trends cannot be overstated. By condensing recipes into short and visually captivating videos, TikTok has made it easier for these trends to spread like wildfire, inspiring countless individuals to try new dishes and experiment with innovative cooking methods.

In addition to fueling creativity and spreading culinary trends, TikTok has played a crucial role in fostering a sense of community and connection among home cooks. The platform has created a space where individuals can share their cooking successes, failures, and discoveries, forming a supportive and interactive community centered around a shared love for food. Through comments, likes, and shares, TikTok users can engage with one another, provide feedback, and offer encouragement, creating a virtual kitchen where people from around the world can connect, learn, and grow together.

Embracing the Ever-Evolving Landscape of Digital Cooking

As we conclude our exploration of TikTok cooking, it is essential to recognize the ever-evolving landscape of digital cooking and embrace the opportunities it presents. TikTok is just one platform among many in the digital realm that has transformed how we approach cooking and food culture. Social media platforms, cooking apps, and online communities continue to shape the way we discover recipes, learn new techniques, and share our culinary adventures.

With the advancements in technology, we can expect further integration of augmented reality (AR) and virtual reality (VR) in the culinary world. These technologies have the potential to revolutionize cooking education by offering immersive experiences, allowing users to virtually step into a kitchen and learn from expert chefs in real-time. Additionally, personalized recipe recommendations, AI-powered cooking assistants, and smart kitchen appliances are likely to become more prevalent, enhancing our cooking experiences and making the process more efficient and enjoyable.

While digital platforms provide a wealth of opportunities, it is crucial to strike a balance between the digital and the tangible. Cooking is not just about following a recipe or creating visually appealing dishes; it is a sensory experience that engages all our senses. The sights, sounds, smells, textures, and tastes of cooking and eating are an integral part of our culinary journey. As we continue to embrace the digital landscape, it is essential to remember the importance of hands-on cooking, family traditions, and the joy of gathering around the dinner table to share a meal.

In conclusion, TikTok cooking has emerged as a dynamic and influential force in the culinary world. It has empowered home cooks, sparked culinary creativity, and fostered a global community of food enthusiasts. By providing a platform for individuals to share their recipes, techniques, and food stories, TikTok has revolutionized the way we learn, engage with, and appreciate cooking.

The impact of TikTok cooking extends beyond the digital realm. As TikTok recipes find their way into kitchens around the world, they have the power to transform everyday cooking experiences. Home cooks are inspired to step out of their culinary comfort zones, try new flavors, and experiment with innovative techniques. The accessibility and simplicity of TikTok recipes make them approachable for individuals of all skill levels, encouraging even novice cooks to explore their culinary potential.

Moreover, TikTok cooking has played a significant role in expanding cultural horizons and promoting inclusivity. The platform has become a melting pot of culinary traditions from various cultures, allowing users to experience global flavors and learn about diverse food cultures. Through TikTok, individuals can connect with others who share their passion for specific cuisines or dietary preferences, fostering a sense of unity and appreciation for culinary diversity.

TikTok cooking has also influenced the way we perceive food aesthetics and presentation. The emphasis on visually appealing dishes has pushed home cooks to elevate their plating skills and explore artistic food presentations. As a result, meals prepared at home are not only delicious but also visually captivating, turning everyday dining into a multisensory experience.

The legacy of TikTok cooking lies in its ability to inspire the next generation of home cooks. The platform has given rise to a new wave of culinary enthusiasts who are eager to experiment, share their creations, and connect with others who share their passion. TikTok has empowered individuals to view cooking as a form of self-expression, creativity, and personal growth. It has encouraged them to take risks, trust their instincts, and explore their unique culinary styles.

As we embrace the legacy of TikTok cooking, it is essential to recognize the importance of balance and moderation in our digital consumption. While TikTok and other digital platforms provide a wealth of inspiration, knowledge, and community, it is crucial to maintain a healthy relationship with technology and prioritize real-life connections. Cooking is not just about the end result; it is about the process, the joy of discovery, and the shared experiences with loved ones.

In conclusion, TikTok cooking has left an indelible mark on the culinary landscape. Its influence on culinary creativity, the global food community, and the accessibility of cooking knowledge cannot be overstated. As we move forward, let us continue to embrace the ever-evolving digital cooking landscape while cherishing the timeless traditions, flavors, and experiences that make cooking a truly enriching and fulfilling endeavor. Whether we're whipping up a viral recipe, exploring new flavors, or simply gathering around the dinner table, TikTok cooking has ignited a passion for culinary exploration that will continue to inspire generations of home cooks to come.

ADDITIONAL RESOURCES AND REFERENCES

Continue your journey in the world of TikTok cooking with these additional resources and references:

1. TikTok App: Download the TikTok app on your smartphone or tablet to start exploring cooking content, following creators, and engaging with the community.

2. TikTok Creator Marketplace: Join the TikTok Creator Marketplace to connect with brands, collaborate on sponsored content, and monetize your cooking videos.

3. TikTok Cooking Hashtags: Discover popular cooking hashtags on TikTok such as #TikTokRecipes, #FoodTikTok, or #CookingTips to find a wide range of recipes, trends, and cooking inspiration.

4. TikTok Cooking Accounts: Follow popular TikTok cooking accounts such as @tiktokfoodie, @foodbyrusk, or @cookingwithayeh for a constant stream of recipe ideas, cooking tips, and food-related content.

5. Online Recipe Websites: Explore dedicated recipe websites such as Bon Appétit, Tasty, or Food Network for additional inspiration and detailed recipes that you can adapt for your TikTok cooking adventures.

6. Cookbooks by TikTok Creators: Some TikTok creators have published cookbooks based on their viral recipes and culinary expertise. Look for cookbooks by creators you admire to explore their recipes in greater detail.

7. Cooking Communities and Forums: Engage with online cooking communities and forums such as Reddit's r/cooking or Facebook cooking groups to connect with like-minded individuals, exchange ideas, and seek advice.

Remember to always credit and attribute original creators when trying out their recipes or techniques. TikTok cooking is a community-driven space that thrives on collaboration, inspiration, and mutual support. Enjoy your culinary journey and continue to explore the diverse flavors, techniques, and trends that TikTok cooking has to offer!

ABOUT THE AUTHOR

I am Annalie Dachs, and I am thrilled to welcome you into the tantalizing world of my TikTok cookbook! As a passionate food enthusiast, home cook, and social media maven, I have dedicated myself to creating a culinary journey like no other.

Born and raised in a small town, I discovered my love for cooking at an early age. The kitchen became my sanctuary, a place where I could experiment, innovate, and let my creativity run wild. But it was the advent of TikTok that truly transformed my culinary adventures into a global sensation.

Harnessing the power of TikTok, I embarked on an extraordinary culinary voyage, taking viewers on a whirlwind tour of mouthwatering recipes, captivating stories, and mouthwatering visuals. With each TikTok video, I strived to transport my audience to the heart of my kitchen, inspiring them to embrace the joy of cooking and sharing meals with loved ones.

Throughout my career, I have developed a keen understanding of how to engage with viewers through the screen, captivating their attention with delectable dishes and infectious energy. My TikTok cookbook is an extension of this passion, allowing me to bring the vibrant TikTok experience to your own kitchen.

In this comprehensive collection, you will discover an array of innovative, yet accessible, recipes that are sure to ignite your taste buds and impress even the most discerning palate. From tantalizing appetizers to sumptuous main courses, and from luscious desserts to refreshing beverages, each dish has been carefully crafted to elevate your culinary repertoire and create unforgettable moments around the table.

But this book is more than just a compilation of recipes; it's a celebration of the TikTok community and the incredible power of social media to connect people through food. I believe that food has the ability to bridge cultures, unite generations, and spark joy, and it is my mission to share that belief with every reader.

Whether you're a seasoned cook or a kitchen novice, my TikTok cookbook will guide you on an adventure filled with culinary delights. Each recipe is accompanied by step-by-step instructions, and helpful tips to ensure your success in recreating these sensational dishes.

So join me on this extraordinary journey as we embrace the flavors of the world, one TikTok recipe at a time. Let's embark on a culinary expedition that will leave you inspired, empowered, and hungry for more. Together, let's make the kitchen the heart of your home and create cherished memories that will last a lifetime.

Thank you for joining me on this delicious adventure!

With love and flavor,
Annalie Dachs

Glossary of TikTok Cooking Terms

To fully immerse yourself in the world of TikTok cooking, familiarize yourself with these common terms and expressions used within the community:

1. FYP (For You Page): The personalized feed on TikTok where users discover content based on their interests and viewing habits.

2. Duet: A feature on TikTok that allows users to create split-screen videos with another user's content, enabling side-by-side comparisons, collaborations, or reactions.

3. POV (Point of View): A storytelling technique used on TikTok where creators assume different perspectives to engage viewers and create relatable content.

4. Recipe Card: A visual representation of a recipe that includes a combination of ingredients, measurements, and instructions. Recipe cards are often shown briefly on-screen during TikTok cooking videos.

5. Food Hack: A clever or unconventional cooking tip or technique that simplifies or enhances the cooking process, resulting in time-saving or flavor-boosting outcomes.

6. Food Trend: A popular recipe, ingredient, or cooking style that experiences a surge in popularity on TikTok, often gaining widespread attention and replication.

Made in the USA
Monee, IL
10 December 2024

73348187R00168